Reclaim the Power of Your Senses

A Complete Guide To Help Business Leaders Build Their Business In Their Own Authentic And Distinctive Way

Benjamin Gifford

1

© Copyrightby All rights reserved.

This eBook is provided with the sole purpose of providing relevant information on a specific topic for which every reasonable effort has been made to ensure that it is both accurate and reasonable. Nevertheless, by purchasing this eBook, you consent to the fact that the author, as well as the publisher, are in no way experts on the topics contained herein, regardless of any claims as such that may be made within. As such, any suggestions or recommendations that are made within are done so purely for entertainment value. It is recommended that you always consult a professional prior to undertaking any of the advice or techniques discussed within.

This is a legally binding declaration that is considered both valid and fair by both the Committee of Publishers Association and the American Bar Association and should be considered as legally binding within the United States.

The reproduction, transmission, and duplication of any of the content found herein, including any specific or extended information, will be done as an illegal act regardless of the end form the information ultimately takes. This includes copied versions of the work, both physical, digital, and audio unless express consent of the Publisher is provided beforehand. Any additional rights reserved.

Furthermore, the information that can be found within the pages described forthwith shall be considered both accurate and truthful when it comes to the recounting of facts. As such, any use, correct or incorrect, of the provided information will render the Publisher free of responsibility as to the actions taken outside of their direct purview. Regardless, there are zero scenarios where the original author or the Publisher can be deemed liable in

2

any fashion for any damages or hardships that may result from any of the information discussed herein.

Additionally, the information in the following pages is intended only for informational purposes and should thus be thought of as universal. As befitting its nature, it is presented without assurance regarding its prolonged validity or interim quality. Trademarks that are mentioned are done without written consent and can in no way be considered an endorsement from the trademark holder.

CHAPTER 1

THE AESTHETIC ADVANTAGE

The term aesthetic is usually used to describe how things look. In business, this means product and packaging design, brand image, and corporate identity. However, this word is much more useful if one wants the full meaning far beyond visual elegance. Aesthetics is the pleasure of us all perceiving objects and experiences through our senses. Aesthetic intelligence Another term we come back to is the ability to understand, interpret, and articulate emotions caused by a particular object or experience.

Aesthetic companies typically use all five senses and provide products or services that are comfortable to buy and consume. In return, consumers do not like to pay a premium for the benefit of these products and services. However, they can see, flavour, taste, smell, hear (sound), and somatosensory (tactile) Preference for the pleasure of sensations including. Aesthetic statements change consumer motivation from functional and transactional to experience-oriented, ambitious, and memorable. For companies, this means higher demand for their products, stronger customer loyalty, and higher value for their shareholders.

In a world where people desire less, crave for more affluent and more meaningful experiences, and have an unprecedented market force to get what they want, the aesthetic value of a company's product or service is essential for its long-term success. Managers, entrepreneurs, and other professionals can harness the power of aesthetics by learning to identify and apply them to their business interests. This critical ability is called aesthetic intelligence. They win when companies involve consumers at an artistic level. In the past, non-luxury sectors that have focused on size, efficiency, and innovation are eroding the value of finance and consumers by rejecting, misunderstanding, or underestimating aesthetics.

Unlike design thinking, which focuses on the problem-solving process and solution-based strategies, the value of business aesthetics is to enhance the human spirit through sensory experiences and delight the opportunity to evoke imagination. When done right, it benefits both businesses and customers. Recently, and for the foreseeable future with money. Computers can solve increasingly functional problems. You cannot and will not find new meaningful ways to reconnect with our humanity.

Automating society means that machines perform today and more and more tasks like analysis, data acquisition, and interpretation, as well as everyday physical tasks and tasks. However, people need to apply their talents and skills to activities where technology cannot be quickly and economically overtaken. This includes the ability to create art, create beauty, and establish deep connections with humans. These are the places where we can go beyond computers.

The retired CEO of Google, remarks, we hope to succeed in the future, and we observe this separation of power and, when necessary, make it possible to operate computers while specializing in doing our best. You have to learn. When striving to mitigate the adverse effects of overproduction and industrial development, the quality, importance, beauty, and durability of goods must be more important than price, accessibility, and availability. The development of aesthetic standards and strategies is essential for the economic and social sustainability of all people and businesses.

IT IS POSSIBLE TO LEARN AESTHETICS

To run an artistic company, managers need to adapt not only to their aesthetics and values but also to their customers' senses and values. Studies show that sentiment and non-analytic thinking affect an estimated 85% of purchase decisions. However, marketers usually focus their efforts on the remaining 15% of the purchase decision, which is a reasonable assessment of functionality.

The value of business aesthetics starts at the top of the leader's own AI, but also depends on the leader's ability to build, support, and maintain the right organization and culture around this aesthetic position. Everyone is born with more artistic skills than he or she uses. Of course, musicians Bob Dylan listens extraordinarily to sound and rhythm, or chefs Wolfgang Puck have the legendary ability to harmonize flavours, textures and tastes, and those who are naturally favoured. Some are talented. But people like Dylan and Puck also need to improve their skills further and develop styles to stay active and relevant in their field, so that their aesthetic advantage is not lost. They also need to adapt to changing preferences on the broader market and modify or optimize individual expressions over time.

After all, classics also need to be modernized to stay relevant. For example, the Louis Vuitton brand, the steamship era that grew up in the first wave of global travel, may have died on a steamship after World War II. Still, the brand is more valuable, influential, and relevant than before. How did you do it? Obtaining the appropriate antithesis among legacy and resurrection, in these rapidly changing times, tradition and heritage values are even more critical. However, brands should not be preserved and presented to museums like works of art. They must still be useful and useful. Marketers need to take the time to understand which aspects of brand heritage are still relevant and which are simply of historical interest. Vuitton, a French luggage maker, introduced a flat-bottomed (stackable) trunk made of canvas (relatively light) and airtight (protected from flood damage) in the mid-19th century. This was a useful and essential innovation for travellers in the steamship era.

The idea of carrying large, stiff luggage in the 21st century is not well suited for modern travel. But the appeal of world travel has never been this exciting. Louis Vuitton has a robust, current, and consistent reference to travel around the world, including advertising campaign photos, store motifs, ornate pop show exhibitions, and curated Voguez and Voyagez, making it a big brand Maintaining relevance. It follows the [brand] adventure from 1854 to the present. However, all of these products are lightweight and compact, making them ideally sized for overhead aircraft containers. Other key companies, such as Apple, Walt Disney Company, Adidas, and Starbucks, are all further enhancing their exceptional aesthetic quality and increasing their desirability while paying attention to legacy and brand codes. None are stagnant.

These companies have similar products to their competitors. Apple smartphones have the same computing power as Samsung. Airbnb, Marriott, and Craigslist offer travelers a competitive accommodation service. Aesthetics is discrimination. That's why some customers are willing to queue up to pay more than $ 1,000 for iPhone X or make a $ 1,000 deposit to be on the Tesla purchase waiting list. Aesthetics explains why Airbnb is by far the largest market for vacation rentals, with both the world's largest hotel group and the established Internet company that has been a market leader for 20 years. The aesthetics of the booking experience are intuitive and attractive. The appearance of the website is clean, elegant, and inherent in terms of functionality. No more than three clicks from the booking. More critical than usability is a website that helps people and encourages them to dream.

The last point about the process of developing and using aesthetic intelligence is what we call artistic empathy: as AI begins to establish its aesthetic sensitivity, it requires as much deep understanding and respect for the sensitivity of others as possible. And unlike ours, it better reflects the market. The fact that there are various types of good taste does not mean that there is no bad taste. "Knowing the difference between good and bad tastes and being sensitive to the good feelings (i.e., aesthetic empathy) of others, imagines, and predicts who will (or will not) respond to your product or service A valuable tool for how.

Understanding how aesthetics can help your business and how to use them effectively and reliably can dramatically increase your chances of survival and longevity. As a prime example, consider Veuve Clicquot, one of the world's most famous champagne brands. A French businessman in the early 19th century, became known as the Great Hall of Champagne due to innovations in the aesthetic expression of champagne. In 1798 she married François Clicquot, the son of the founder of Maison Clicquot. François shared the passion and knowledge of champagne with his wife. When she became a widow at the age of 27 in 1805, she was able to run a business. The business continued to prosper under her leadership.

Madam Clicquot not only saved the family business but improved it by developing a new production technique called puzzles that dramatically improved the taste and visual appeal of champagne. She has developed a method to combat the unpleasant appearance of sediment deposited on the bottom of the bottle. This technique is still used by winegrowers today. Madame Clicquot has also innovated the first blend of rose champagne. Rose champagne is a fascinating pink that is popular for weddings and special occasions around the world. The yellow-yellow label, a signature of Clicquot since 1772, is a powerful visual marker of brand tradition and personality. Madame Clicquot used her aesthetic intelligence to improve existing products, create special ones, and make it timeless. The power of a robust artistic strategy has built her company one of the world's leading champagne brands. However, Mrs. Clicquot was not born with the knowledge of the wine industry and did not go to college to study design. Instead, she saw with her husband and learned to trust her instinct on what was right about the product and what would be better. Here, the book starts with the idea that you can learn AI.

Art historian Maxwell L. Anderson states that, as Madame Clicquot showed, developing AI does not require formal training or growth in a sophisticated environment, but it certainly does provide the foundation. Claim to be useful. According to Dr. Anderson is a skill that anyone can develop. If you are passionate about cooking, you may have a sophisticated instinct for quality food. The cyclist brings the same rigor to his judgment on bicycles—oil and acrylic painters of certain brands. According to Anderson, they should be able to transfer these skills and develop their art and design judgment. Chef's favorite Le Creuset kitchenware follows the same principles of excellent craftsmanship as other luxury goods. Learn how to recognize and use this ability to distinguish between making objects and experiences fun in other areas. This is the first step to foster AI. Practice leads to polishing. Once you recognize the quality, resist the urge to copy others. Authenticity and originality are essential to long-term aesthetic results, especially in business. Fast fashion brands can create patterns, styles, and silhouettes similar to the coveted high-end designer goods, but the value of these replicas diminishes with each wear. Like new cars, discounts have little resale value. Helms Birkin bags, on the other hand, are often auctioned at prices much higher than the original retail price.

Take creative and visionary people to the executive suite, give them the same place at the table, and empower them to do their best. Do not justify all decisions in financial calculations. For businessmen like David Rubenstein, being surrounded by aesthetically intelligent people is especially important. Given his position, he may not need to have a strong sense of aesthetic himself. Aesthetic value is not limited to design-oriented companies in areas such as beauty and fashion. Making connections between people is a complex task and has far-reaching implications. It can be done through aesthetics. Hopefully, it will lead to a more luxurious brand experience. It is the responsibility of the creator to harmonize his thoughts with motifs that are worth personally experiencing deeply. Modern consumers who are no longer interested in the accumulation of material possessions are looking for depth and meaning. That's why a tolerable brand makes sense, is emotional, and inspires imagination. Your drivers are far beyond commercial motivation. They strive to unite and delight generations who are impressed with their products and services. Aesthetically productive companies must be built on a bright and stable foundation. Ultimately, it challenges, empowers, and appeals to customers. You don't need to see or treat your customers merely wanting to consume them, but eventually, you want to feel alive.

CHAPTER 2

SENSES

As mentioned in this book, about 85% of consumers' purchasing decisions depend on how they feel about the product or service (aesthetic pleasure). Only 15% is based on a conscious and rational assessment of product features and functions. Ironically, marketers are up to 100% focused on developing, building and promoting product features. As eternal as the commodity or co-operation is functioning, companies that stimulate the senses and find ways to create associative or emotional connections have long-term value.

CREATIVITY AND PSYCHOLOGY OF SENSATION

Sensations are accessed through a series of biological and neurological activities that are perceived and identified by the brain and then respond to relevant memories that remind people, places, or events. Our aesthetics are highly dependent on how we interpret sensory experiences. It's not commonplace, especially when creating lessons and moments that involve people.

Sound first reaches the brain by vibrating the eardrum toward the ear canal. Vibration is transmitted to the co cow through the ossicles. Due to the wave of the sound, the liquid in the cow moves and the hair cells bend. Hair cells generate nerve signals that the auditory nerve picks up. The hair cells at one end of the co cow transmit bass sound information, and the hair cells at the other end communicate treble sound details. The auditory nerve sends signals to the brain. In mind, signals are interpreted as loud or soft, calming or abrasive. Humans respond to certain sounds. The sound of the jackhammer is annoying and annoying, forcing you to close windows and throb across the street. However, the sound of a crying baby is intolerable, ideally crying with the sound source. Find a comfortable child. Barring dogs is seen as a note, and laughing tells us to relax and take part in the fun.

The smell is a chemical process, and our nasal receptors and nerves identify chemicals in the environment, which can be benign, comfortable, or repellent. Our sense of smell also relates to the olfactory bulb, one of the structures of the limbic system, the old part of the human brain. Our understanding of smell is rooted in the natural part of the brain, part of the survival mechanism. The olfaction is not connected by the thalamus, which integrates all other sensory information. The odour is sent directly to the amygdala and the hypothalamus. None of our other senses has such a direct connection to the area of the brain responsible for processing emotions, associative learning, and memory. The scent of freshly cut grass is reminiscent of early summer. Citrus fruits, especially lemons, represent cleanliness. The pine reminds us of a festive winter vacation. As the findings show, all three fragrances make us happy. Coffee-like aromas can help solve analytical problems better.

Touch is part of the somatosensory system and an extensive and diverse network of receptors and processing centres that help to perceive the pleasant sensations, temperatures and pain that are processed in the parietal lobe of the cerebral cortex. These sensory receptors cover the skin and epithelium, skeletal muscle, bones and joints, internal organs and even the cardiovascular system. Cashmere conveys a feeling of luxurious comfort. The refreshing taste of the tightly woven percale leaf conveys a sense of elegance and order. Rough oak tables convey a feeling of strength and durability.

The view is the predominant sense of the post-industrial age, in which visual perception consists of perceiving light, colour, shape, movement and everything else in our environment. Of course, what we see is interpreted in the brain, but specific colours and configurations can manipulate it. In the west, red often means standstill, blood or gender. Yellow means happy and sunshine. White means purity and cleanliness. And green means freshness and nature.

Taste or taste is the ability to recognize the feeling of a substance. In humans (and other vertebrates) the taste often has a less perceived smell than the perception of the flavour in the brain. It is a function of the central nervous system. Our taste receptors are located on the surface of the tongue, soft palate, pharynx and epiglottis epithelium. Traditionally we have defined four primary taste sensations: sweet, salty, sour and bitter. The fifth sensation, called Umami, is a new sensation that has been added to the traditional four. The sweet taste is related to fun and enjoyment (ice cream, chocolate), flavour with warmth and comfort (homemade pasta, roast chicken, vegetable soup), strength and Umami (parmesan, tomatoes, mushrooms, beef).

THE INFLUENCE OF HALO

Aesthetic pleasure is the deep satisfaction or pleasure felt when a sensation (at least three of the five are victorious) is awake, concerning a particular product, a specific brand, a particular service, or a specific experience is. Interestingly, this form of pleasure consumes not only a product or service but also the same memory that evokes a sense when we handle it, due to the combination of expectation and memory of experience using the product or service. Treat the sensory elements of the product that you can enjoy. Studies show that about 50% of consumer pleasure is related to expectations and memories (the rest of past sensory experiences). The other fifty per cent is associated with direct experience (five senses work together and keep people busy at this time).

Although it does not explain how a company can spread a company's financial success, the experience is a continuum that includes the memory of the lead, the background, and what repeatedly informs the point. The original example is birth. The stimulating expectations of the baby and the memory of how wonderful the newborn felt and smelled often contrasted with the intolerable pain of contraction during actual childbirth. This pain can be forgiven when distant memories are reached or when the second baby's expectations come, and the excitement and expectations rise again. Remember to have a delicious meal. Eating is fun, but remembering the next day is part of the experience, and thinking and planning to eat at the same restaurant in the future. The same is true for roller coaster vehicles. Not only the thrill of going out but also the connection to carnivals and parks with family and friends, the memory of feelings when we hit the truck up and down is significant,

Family trips at Disney World are another prime example of the halo effect. The experience of being at a theme park is generally enjoyable, but it's not without its drawbacks, such as the unbearably hot and humid conditions of Orlando. Sharp long lines that lead to the most popular trips, especially at peak times. The high cost of meals on the premises. However, when asked to explain Disney's vacation, most of us thought of a smile on a child's face, the thrill of embracing Mickey, the magic of seeing a princess stroll through her kingdom, and colourful, fun entertainment Flood. As families prepare for their upcoming Disney World vacation, we are increasingly excited to experience the latest rides and meet the latest characters. Just remembering the pleasures, you got from your last visit, it's not the excruciating heat of Orlando or the monotony of waiting for the Astro Orbiter to spin. Disney World provides such a magical and unforgettable experience, allowing people to be involved in all senses and emotions. Seven Other consumer experiences can offer equally immersive opportunities by being able to see, feel, hear, taste, and smell deeply personal things. Personal territory has benefits. The theme parks (and companies) are significant, but the lessons taught by Disney World are beyond the scale. Disney has found a way to discover the brand and strip that layer for customers known as guests.

Regrettably, the halo effect doesn't take into account the customer experience from start to finish, so companies are always wrong. For example, clothing stores and boutiques welcome you and make the entrance comfortable and attractive. A salesperson can help me without being obedient. However, paying for items can be a hassle, and deliveries that even high-end department stores are perceived as red and indifferent can leave unpleasant or at least unobtrusive memories. Retailers, in particular, can make the shopping experience more enjoyable, exciting and memorable.

The traditional retail store is not dead but lost. They are boilerplate and even worse are unforgettable. How can retailers impress their customers better, preferably very positively? For starters, employees can greet them and say goodbye when they enter the store. They were able to send handwritten notes to the best customers and show their attention and appreciation. While such efforts may seem trivial, do not underestimate the impact of personal records on people. Research conducted at the University of Texas found that those who were recognized felt much happier than researchers had expected. On average, study participants took less than 5 minutes to write a letter. Retailers can also include small gifts that are not sold in stores but are complementary and original at the time of purchase. B. Perfume samples, potpourri or confectionery. People also call and thank customers with names that are readily available on credit cards and claim to remember the names of those who return. Such gestures are smooth and practically inexpensive.

Bite Beauty calls the store a lipstick lab, and stores in New York, Los Angeles, San Francisco and Toronto exemplify a clean, elegant lab-like appearance while being fashionable and comfortable. With a long shiny countertop, you can raise the chair while allowing technicians to create custom colours together. The purchase of lipstick is personal and unique. That is in contrast to many shopping experiences where people feel abandoned in large stores or ignored by untrained and indifferent staff. Not only for purchasing power but also personality, sellers need to rethink their return to courteous service where they are genuinely interested in their customers. Successful [retail] technology does not leave people behind or increase efficiency, but it facilitates transactions and facilitates person-to-person interaction. This connection can be achieved by dealing with feelings. Bite turns what is an essential and everyday beauty product for many into a creative and interactive experience enhanced by store design, lighting, atmosphere and staff.

People especially love shopping at the Joe Malone fragrance store because it's sensory appealing, and everything feels special. Vendors are well trained and talk about fragrances professionally and generously. Buyers are encouraged to try as much perfume as they like and enjoy the experience of comparing scents. The point of purchase is the most exciting part of Joe Malone Travel. When items such as gifts are packaged and presented, the brand flourishes at checkout. The products are carefully wrapped in grosgrain boxes, packed in luxurious shopping bags, and gorgeously handed. When you get home, open the gift and proudly place it on your dresser or desk to continue the experience.

THE SHAPE OF GOOD TASTE AND SOUND

The taste of cooking does not mean that it comes out as frequently as the other four senses. However, it is essential for everyone involved in eating and drinking to understand the taste correctly. Even if the product is made with the freshest and highest quality ingredients, other factors can be a disaster for even the most delicious meals, snacks and cocktails. Start with something as simple as a glass of wine. The thinner the lens, the better the wine tastes, and it is not done. It is in science. According to chemists, the rise in steam from wine differs from the specific shape and thickness of the glass, which can have a positive or negative effect on the taste of the wine. It is widely believed that champagne tastes best from the long, high flutes, and that foam quickly falls off of the old-fashioned (but still attractive) coupe.

In reality, the excellent champagne taste is best when served in a good quality thin white wine glass. Restaurants (and others) that serve fine champagne on a flute or coupe will undermine the drinking experience. One of the reasons for the love of champagne is that the whistle keeps the wine whisked, says Seth Box, retail director at Hennessy, which owns the world's best champagne brand. However, flutes prevent you from experiencing the scent of wine, which is part of the tasting experience. You can't put your nose in a narrow pipe, Box Notes.

THE GRACE OF UGLINESS

The activation of sensations to achieve aesthetic pleasure does not only derive from the standard movement of beauty and comfort. It also comes from many repulsive experiences that seem to be many or scary. The French have the word Jolly Reid, which is very hard and means to represent the idea best. People are attracted to things that repel. Of course, but not always, this concept explains why we are satisfied with the weird satisfaction of the roller coaster of the heavy metal band Anthrax, the horror movie The Exorcist and Dreamworlds Tower of Terror. Even fashion can touch and attract joy through our senses.

Gucci's recent success in ugly fashion has also become apparent. Alessandro Michele, who took over Gucci in 2015, is also known for his unlimited anti-beauty approach to prints, patterns and graphics. A clear path to him, chic and nerdy, using quirky and surprising patterns and colours, may seem purist-like and tasteless to purists. However, for many others, its design has created a new way to access European luxury and has permitted to express people in unconventional and unusual ways. He chose a category, high fashion, which was reasonably fun and bound by rules, and made it fun and creative again. Michelle's general design ethic is that more is more. That is more colours, more patterns, more textures.

His designs are better for strangers. Because they offer all kinds of ways to connect with people through sensations, some models are reminiscent of what we consider simpler due to the retro feel of the 60s, 70s, and even the 80s. In the romantic past, we feel happy and safe even when we were not there at the time (as in Gucci's youngest customer). This spirit is from famous and successful sneakers, very colourful knitwear, shoes, handbags, wallets, backpacks, sweaters, denim shorts, hoodies, bomber jackets and scarves for jeweler. The featured puppy illustration is featured by an artist named Helen Downey, also known as an unskilled worker. He gave Michelle two pillows decorated with

Boston's two Boss Terrier and Ortho graphics. This is a Michele classic. Inspired by artists and translated into surprises and fun consumer goods. But does it define the traditional notion of beauty in fashion? Not at all. There are edgy designs, and they are challenging.

As long as ugly fashion is based on attractive properties, such as charm and quirkiness. Ugliness is never a good thing, even if it's means if it's based on real traits like mean and horny. Consider the difference between a goofy pug and a roaring bloodthirsty pit bull. Most people think the first photo is cute (although it may be dirty anyway) and the second photo is adorable. Gucci's blunder in a black sweater is a classic example. In February 2019, the company commemorated an $ 890 black shirt with red lips woven around the mouth opening of the wearer. Critics of the sweater noted that if the company employed more colored personnel in the design and marketing departments, the jerseys would have been classified as inappropriate before being made.

ACTIVATE AND REACTIVATE: SENSORY MARKETING

Emotions may be fleeting, but related feelings last longer. Therefore, marketers need to understand the perceived impact on customers before, during, and after the experience. Everything is essential when thinking about how to involve people's senses. Sensory engagement must be active. The sensations do not need to be as comfortable as before, but they should not be uncomfortable. Stomach roller coaster rides, Gucci crazy fashion, and loud heavy metal music all have enthusiastic fans. They understand their core components and know-how sharp senses can deal with them, but for others, it may be an unpleasant sensation.

A typical example is a Bloomingdale sales representative who sprinkles perfume, whether they like the customer or not. Perhaps the fragrance may smell good, but it may not, but it is an unpleasant experience when imposed very aggressively on buyers. Today, the approach to selling perfume in department stores has changed dramatically as retailers understand that technology affects not only the senses but also the people. Today, many retailers are training salespeople to ask their customers for their favourite scents, ask for answers, and then try the fragrances that suit their tastes.

Rolls-Royce noticed that the smell was beneficial as it modified the manufacturing method and began using leather-based plastic instead of wood for some parts of the vehicle. Customers didn't like the smell of plastic. It was not the luxury new car smell they were expecting from an automaker. Sales fell. Rolls-Royce was smart enough to ask customers why they rejected the new model. Customers said the old models smelled tasty and woody, but the new cars smelled of the plastic used to make them. One of the few components of the new model (window switches and dash switches also felt lighter due to the use of lighter materials) had an impact on sales but was significant. People's expectations for a product related to how they sensibly interact with the product. Rolls-Royce addresses this problem by hiring a smell expert, mimicking the woody smell of old cars, and developing a scent that uses the smell of the 1965 Rolls-Royce Silver Cloud as a model. The scent was applied to new car interiors after manufacture.

The aroma is also cultural. When dealing with customers, companies need to consider who is buying and what olfactory expectations they have. For Americans, the smell of clean tide detergents is contrasting, according to Olivia Jezler, head of Future of Smer, a fragrance expert and dedicated to flavour science, psychology and flavour design. Besides, she says the idea of a clean smell is in China or India. Chinese medicine, often based on herbs, affects cleansing purposes, as well as Ayurvedic medicine in India. People in these countries' associate cleanliness with soil and grass odours more than Americans who tend to combine freshness with a floral scent.

Starbucks has also found that odours are beneficial. Lessons learned when an unwanted and unexpected smell in the form of a breakfast roll, like Rolls-Royce, was brought into the store. The decline in patron sales in 2008 was directly related to the smell of sandwiches. It created a royalist. It disrupted the aroma of coffee that enthusiasts had hoped and enjoyed, and ultimately spoiled the overall store experience. The lunch was withdrawn, re-formulated and returned without an unpleasant odour.

INCONSPICUOUS PATTERN AND ENHANCED COMFORT

Best-in-class companies often also provide an impactful but undetected sensory experience. This is called an invisible design. The elements may not be distinct but have little or no value. Note that all lipsticks are made from the same essential ingredients. Why do women pay six times more than Chanel Rouge Allure Velvet lipstick ($ 37) sold at Neiman Marcus than LeBron Cherry's super gloss lipstick ($ 6.02) sold at Wal-Mart? Women may say that they like the way lipstick in Chanel lasts or how long it lasts, but the truth is that they prefer the aesthetic experience of using more expensive lipsticks. The quality of the wax is, of course, equal to the shade of red.

User pleasure can be enhanced by the weight of the Chanel cylinder, the lustre of the metal rims, or the elegantly engraved double C logo on the cap. Even the experience of buying Chanel lipstick is rarer than going to a darkly lit drugstore, pulling out a transparent and tamper-evident plastic package from a luggage rack, and having to wait for the cashier to call you. A luxurious, fun buy. LeBron and its drugstore partners claim that they can learn much from Chanel about maintaining aesthetic currencies and increasing sales without necessarily increasing costs or prices.

By investing a few extra pence per unit, Revlon could transform the secondary packaging and wrap the lipstick in a small matchbox that felt more exclusive and worthy of a gift. (Regarding the sale of beauty products, you must consider the gift ceremony.) LeBron can also engrave its name or logo on the wax of the stick. For Chanel, this design element means that real applications will feel less common and more identifiable. LeBron may also consider restructuring the language of advertising. Currently, it focuses on functionality (wax-free gel technology), uses clichés and kitsch expressions (at-a-glance), and lacks attractive visual cues—a more powerful original photographic style for Chanel ads. Concerning merchandising, LeBron displays items in collections (ColorStay, PhotoReady) or appearances (smoky eyes, gay lockers) and cannot show them in categories (lipstick, mascara). This will prevent consumers from purchasing individual (problem-solving) items or buying seasonal sets or overall styles. Above all, consumers will be able to dream. When it comes to makeup, consumers buy experiences that are accessible through a variety of products that look personal and proprietary.

SOUND EFFECTS AND OUR PREFERENCES

Sound affects us in four ways. The first is physiological. Sirens, fighting humans, hearing a dog snarl will have a fighting or flying response, while soothing sounds of ocean waves and birdsong will calm down and reduce heart rate. Indicates that things are safe (worry if the bird stops singing). The second is psychological. For example, music affects our emotional state. Sad music makes us depressed, and fast music makes us happy. Natural noise also affects emotions. Birds singing the same song brings us joy and physiological comfort. The third way that sound affects us is cognition. People working in open-plan offices with many workers are 66% less productive than those with private and quiet offices. Open-plan offices have gained popularity during the tech boom, and some companies are still at a disadvantage.

The fourth way sound affects us in action. If you hear fast music while driving, you can step on the accelerator. Listen to Pachelbel's Canon, and you can work in a speed zone of 45 mph and 55 mph. The tone determines what we eat. Studies show that people are more likely to choose sugar and high-calorie snacks and junk food when surrounded by loud music and healthier products when listening to soft and quiet music.

Dipayan Biswa, professor of economics and marketing at the University of South Florida in Tampa, says loud music is more exciting, physically excited, unrestrained, and tends to choose something more generous. Low music makes us more relaxed and mindful and tends to choose something suitable for us in the long run.

We usually tend to stay away from unpleasant noises (e.g., construction teams blasting on city sidewalks) and hear soothing sounds (e.g., ice cream truck ringing). Unfortunately, lousy noise can have a detrimental effect on retail space (and other commercial spaces). Approximately 30% of people will open a store if it contains unpleasant noise.

Supermarkets often use elevator music to slow down, last, and even buy. Up-tempo music is commonly used in restaurants to enter and exit, to energize both guests and staff and to quickly turntables. However, if the beat is bothersome, you can skip the jump altogether. In a classic French restaurant, you can set the mood and pace by playing chanties with Piaf in the back. However, if the volume is too loud to talk or hear with peers, an Italian location where Frank Sinatra plays quietly may win. Shops that make music out loud can hurt the enjoyment of browsing and trying on, and provide poor service to themselves and their customers.

CHAPTER 3

CRACKING THE CODE

> ➤ **KNOW YOUREMOTIONAL TRIGGERSAND BRAND'S SENSORIAL CUES**

The Nokia ringtone, also known as Grande Valse, was the first ringtone to be identified on a cell phone. It was introduced by the Finnish company in the early 90s and came from the composition of the Spanish composer Francisco Tarrega for solo guitar from 1902. Today it is played 20,000 times per second on mobile phones worldwide. Tapio Hakanen, Head of Sound Design at Nokia, told reporters in 2014. Today's tones are less pronounced, but the use of soft acoustic guitars for ringtones was infrequent at first. It reflected the human aspect of the motto that connects the people of Nokia. It was fresh at the time. In a way, the popularity of this ring tone signalled the foresight of the ultimate performance of mobile devices to bring people around the world and use technology to advance humanity.

A good business is built with thousands of components, but a good brand is made with just a handful of robust code. Grande Valse has probably become one of the essential Nokia brand codes. What is the brand code? They are clear and unambiguous identifications or hallmarks of the brand, which summarize their philosophical and aesthetic aspects. Do not confuse the brand code with the brand logo. However, a symbolic logo can be one of many different types of code. The brand code differs from the brand DNA, which is usually based on factors such as brand history, value and social purpose (or mission) since DNA is conceptual in nature and not sensory. Perhaps most importantly, while the code stands out from the brand's salable products, it consciously and subconsciously connects consumers to the ideas, memories, and emotions that these products create, and it also encourages consumers to buy.

Spatially, code can be seen, felt, heard and even experienced. In fact, they are almost everywhere in products, products and products. For example, a strong slogan can create an emotionally charged connection that stimulates the desire for related products. For instance, Folger is the best part of awakening, Coca-Cola likes to teach the song to the world, and Meow, Meow, Meow, Meow, Meow in Meow Mix evoke the morning time and the pleasant feeling of a fresh start. Unity and community. And the sweetness and charm of the pet you love. Chords found in sounds like Nokia songs, Ho-ho-ho by Jolly Green Giant or MGM lion tones also create strong associations.

Robust visual codes can be found in certain colour uses and ownership such as Harvard Crimson Red, Cadbury Royal Purple and Veuve Clicquot's Yolk Yellow. Ms. Lauder chose a light greenish-blue shade for the skincare glass to encourage it to blend well into the customer's bathroom decor and proudly show the cream on the counter. But it also made her look at the elegance that made her glasses easily recognizable from a distance and reminded of the use of the fabulous European chinoiserie. Today, the brand uses a broader range of shades, from copper brown to shiny white, but the original blue remains for some of the best-known creams and lotions.

The code is also found in the room and building designs. B. Backlit apple. It stands out and is built into the Apple Store wall. Besides, the Apple Store is easily recognized by spacious rooms, floor-to-ceiling glass facades, and front hangar doors. These factors not only distinguish Apple from nearby stores, but also blur the distinction between inside and outside, and draw people's attention to the product display, which is the star of the Apple stage. Interestingly, other retailers tend to fail when trying to copy Apple's design approach. Because they feel their imitation business is fake and uninspired.

The code served the company as long as US consumers wanted consistency and predictability and wanted to see the country by driving long distances inside the company. Johnson, after a long day of driving and seeing new places, realized that imaginary comfort (without cleaning up) from home was warmly accepted. For this reason, new restaurants were modeled on New England churches or the town hall with gable or wing roofs and domes. The New England City Hall itself was a code borrowed by Johnson to show welcome, security, and traditional hospitality. According to Langdon, the shingles on the porcelain and metal roofs are painted orange to attract the attention of distant drivers. But when American desires changed, HoJo was no different from them, and the company lost its lead. Andrew King, a professor at the Tuck School of Business at Dartmouth University, and Brazier Bataltok Tof, a Ph.D. student at the University of British Columbia in Vancouver, ultimately forced cleanup with basic economics.

Consumers generally buy products and services based on how they feel about these offers. If a proposal cannot keep up with the changing desires of consumers, businesses will fail. HoJo's is a classic example. It is challenging for a company to create emotions through product design alone. Brand codes provide much more meaning and emotional resonance than individual products. They are one of the brand's most valuable assets, as they create a strong and lasting passionate connection between people and products. In essence, they are the root of the desirability of a product, or what economists call demand.

HOW CODES EVOLVE

The code evolves and evolves organically, slowly, and unintentionally. Usually, they emanate from the founder of the company and his or her basic principles and personal preferences. The brand code itself is not created as a code. They are a by-product of a broader creative process. If the system is well-designed and consistently integrated into the brand development effort, it will become the most recognizable element of the brand. It will continue to show meaningful and memorable stories about the brand's story, its experience, and the product You. In essence, the code leverages our desires and creates a dreamy myth bubble.

Over time, the myth that the code suggests will be integrated with the brand. Systems are abbreviated narratives that are far more emotionally compelling than the product itself. For example, one of the most prominent codes of the French luxury brand Herm is the Duc carriage logo painted by a horse. The company was founded by Thierry Hermes in Paris in the 1800s as a harness workshop to serve European aristocrats. Hermes has created the finest forged harnesses and reins for the transportation industry. So, Ma was really a brand client. Two centuries later, the code still represents Hermes' commitment to traditional European craftsmanship and rare but modest luxury.

In general, the richer the heritage and the deeper the archive, the more powerful and persistent the code is. When looking at a mature brand, ask yourself: What did the founders basically believe in their business proposals? How do these principles relate to the context in which the business is deployed (i.e., time/location / other variables), and how does the code stay relevant through changes in time, culture, and the environment?

However, young companies and start-ups also have the heritage. For new companies, context is often found in the culture. For example, Amazon.com has accessibility, value, corporate value, and convenience.

PRECISE AND SPECIFIC

Robust code is never seen in the general description, but it can be found in an exact and concrete explanation. For example, UPS is marked with the trademark Pullman Brown, not brown. 3M post-it notes are not yellow. It is Canary Yellow. Hermes has a distinctive shade of burnt orange. Louis Vuitton possesses a particular shade of brown: old burgundy and dirt. Tiffany's color is not just blue. It is neither navy, sky blue, or blue-green. Robin's egg blue. No. 1837 on the Pantone Matching System chart. Tiffany began using the distinctive shade of Robin's egg blue on the cover of the Blue Book in 1845, less than ten years after its foundation. That's almost two centuries of branding.

The same is valid for logo codes. Starbucks does not use ordinary old mermaids with one tail. It uses a green illustrated siren with two tails inspired by an ancient Nordic woodcut. (The name Starbucks comes from the character of Harman Melville's famous novel "Movie Dick." Starbucks was the first companion of Captain Ahab's ship, Pecod. Starbucks Global Creative Studios, the most prominent symbol of our brand is the relationship between Starbucks and coffee: First, the company was founded in Seattle, close to Puget Sound, and has strong ties to water, and second, coffee beans are in Ethiopia. Travel long distances from exotic and distant locations, such as Kenya and Colombia, and arrive in large container ships. According to myths, mermaids are also born from exotic places, travel the open ocean, Third, the Greek god In, Starbucks in the same way as to tempt coffee lovers, that siren was lured sailors. Siren concrete depiction of is something to remember when you think about Starbucks.

OWNABLE

The meaningful and robust specialty of the code is the reason why many companies and institutions protect against infringements, legally register their brands, and eagerly persecute those who try to steal them for their own benefit. This brings the next function of robust code: ownership.

Despite the limitations of intellectual property, robust code cannot only be duplicated by others. And even if it is reproduced, it is still closely related to the original brand owner. Imagine a graphic mouse-ear used by Walt Disney, a Neuschwanstein-inspired castle, or an Anthora coffee mug for two used by a Greek diner. A font that resembles Greek letters and has a blue and white color scheme inspired by the Greek flag. Think of a ring on the Dutch oven lid from Le Creuset. In all these cases, the house rules are profound, e.g., B. with a mouse, a lock, a paper coffee cup, or an enameled cast iron pot and typical woven leather chairs from Bottega Veneta or molded plastic chairs from Charles and Ray Eames and forever associated with the brand that originally placed it on the card.

The code is very closely linked to the brand. So, when people get out of context or used by other brands, the link to the original brand is secure and is strictly protected by the original owner. Disney mouse ears are more than Mickey. It conveys playful and bizarre sensations, childhood dreams, innocence, and charm. In 2014, the company sued a famous DJ wearing a mouse ear helmet on live shows around the world. According to Disney, DJ Joel Zimmerman, known as Deadmau5, uses a logo that resembles the ears of a Disney mouse, but using the Zimmerman icon is precisely the opposite of the story Disney wants to tell. The case was settled in 2015, and DJs use large mouse ears as part of the brand.

TIME-TESTED

Robust code has evolved and, as mentioned, is generally not considered code. The most robust system evolves over time and rarely changes. If they change, the changes are conservative and incremental. Chanel's classic tweed jacket didn't start as a brand code, but it has undoubtedly developed into a brand code and continues to be a reliable identifier for the brand. The fabric itself was commissioned by Coco Chanel in 1924 and was inspired by the sports equipment that her then handsome Duke of Westminster wore. Chanel was responsible for making the first Tweed at a Scottish factory and produced a variety of sportswear, including suits and coats. However, it wasn't until 1954 that Tweed really became unique when she used it in today's Chanel jacket.

Fashion claims that nothing is more iconic than this classic jacket, with woven, real buttonholes and a small metal chain that is sewn on the inside of the bottom so that it fits the body properly. Although the jacket design has kept pace with the times in terms of fresh colors and slight changes in cuts, the basic silhouette remains close enough to the original form 1954 to be easily recognizable. It was an impressive example of chic modernity and simplicity back then but still is today. Even in the over-owned 1980s, it was a staple in fashionista cabinets. You can always find classic Chanel tweed jackets on the Chanel e-commerce website. Suits continue to be overpriced in the secondary market. The basic design and construction of the coat have not changed significantly since it was first conceived. The jacket sends a strong message. The person who wears it is rich, appropriate, has great taste, and understands quality. There's a lot to tell you about a jacket. The power of the cable, as well as the style, are part of why this jacket has been knocked off by countless other brands and manufacturers.

Proven code is more than just fashion. Legacy food companies use the strength of their standards. It is mentioned Jolly Green Giant Hohoho earlier. Chants and jingles have long been associated with frozen peas and vegetables. The giant Ho-ho-ho has not changed since its introduction in 1925, but the giants themselves have been subtly modernized since then. It got bigger, looked better, and became more environmentally friendly. Despite the improvements, he was immediately recognized as the company's mascot and continues to challenge this category as a large and bright vegetable code. Even if they end up buying a different brand, flashes of the Jolly Green Giant are forever etched in the minds of many shoppers in the frozen food aisle.

RELEVANT

Robust code is related to other aspects of the brand. They were not developed independently but feel authentic and reliable. For example, Tiffany Blue, a combination of blue and green, gives a fresh and soothing feeling. And it is timeless and never out of place. Color is associated with calm, peace, prosperity, and femininity. All of this connects seamlessly with the company's essential salable products, including jewelry, especially exquisitely designed household items such as diamonds, precious metals, crystals, and ceramics.

Tiffany has a profound legacy to build, but it 'sits still somehow modern and relevant. The brand code should not be treated as a museum piece of art. They even have to be useful and applicable. Marketers need to take the time to understand which aspects of brand heritage are actually still very relevant and which characters are simply historically interesting. As mentioned earlier, the Louis Vuitton brand, for example, matured during the rise of the steamship era, the first significant wave of international travel. Vuitton, a French luggage manufacturer, introduced a trunk with a flat bottom (stackable), canvas (relatively light), and airtight (flood protected) in the mid-19th century.

Louis Vuitton canvas materials were practical and light, most of which were perfect for modern steamboat travel. LV has always been a luxury and has long been preferred by the rich. It is still relevant for luxury travelers today. However, as trips around the world become more desirable, exciting, and accessible to more people, Louis Vuitton has successfully expanded its base and is an ambitious brand for more than one boar-rich jet setter. and Voyagez pop-ups that are adventurous to send powerful, modern, and consistent messages that lead to travel. [brand] from 1854 until today.

WHEN GOOD CODES GO BAD

Betty Crocker's brand would have suffered if she had continued to rely on the clichés of highly domesticated middle-aged American white women. This is the wrong code of the 21st century. One of the biggest disasters in overall coding is in physical stores. Department stores fromMacy's to Dillard, in particular, have stuck to the same traditional, uninspired approach to store design for decades. Of course, they feel dated, homogeneous, and boring. Mainly, the lack of an associated code wipes out the emotional ties that consumers once felt, and another reason many traditional retailers crave air, and Claire, Bonton, sports authorities, 4, toys, etc. have filed for bankruptcy.

Retailers are not irrelevant. It is not. Older brands like Louis Vuitton and Gucci have found a way to stay relevant. ABC Carpet & Home, one of the favorite shops in New York, creates a theater feel for houses and decorations in a dramatic atmosphere. The interior of the flagship store resembles a charming boutique street where you can search for events. The Parisian retail store Le Bon March (one of the favorite stores) keeps its iconic escalator design and the impressive culinary shop window La GrandeÉpiceriede Paris, but its old code Illuminating, architecturally inspiring spaces keep finding new ways to turn into unique and creative shopping moments. Le Bon Marché is said to be the first department store in the world to open in Paris in 1852 by the French entrepreneur and retailer Aristide Bousseau and his wife, Marguerite. They wanted to open a new kind of business that stimulates all the senses. The massive iteration of the Parisian company was designed by architect Louis-Charles Boileau and engineer Gustave Eiffel (yes, his Eiffel). Boucicaut is also innovative by today's standards, talks to customers, and develops many sensory experiences that have made the business a success. Different prices and entertainment for children. Seasonal sales, including a mail-order catalog (actually the world's first) and white bedding sales that take place after Christmas when traffic has decreased. The store continues to surprise locals and tourists with magical displays, curated departments, magnificent architecture, and furnishings.

There are ways that retailers can be successful. People always feel, touch, and feel the need to sniff, and retailers offer a place where they can do so. Retail is a place where products and experts (salespeople) can engage customers' senses with the unique, surprising, and useful. That's what retail should strive for.

MINING FOR CODES

Code comes from expressions and actions that are proven over time to be consistent, authentic, and emotionally tenacious. Whether your company is 100 years old or five years old, for anyone trying to reveal the code, the first step is to do what I call a brand audit. Jump into the archive. Of course, the deeper your legacy, the more work you have to do. For established companies, looking back at the files, as fashion houses often do, can be a remarkable experience. This is not only how your product was historically made and sold, but also why it was made and sold, how its expression was influenced by the times, and above all, an immersive sense of how it has evolved throughout history. Who is the founder? How was he or she influenced by the times? What other forces worked? How has your brand evolved in a changing context and impact? What was the defining moment of the brand? From now on, you can see the pattern appear. You can see which expressions of the brand continue to resonate, which emotions do not resonate, and how the company's leadership, culture, and market have responded to various cues in the process.

The archive may contain samples or images of the product design (preferably presented in chronological order so that auditors can see how the model has evolved). However, you must also include other visible elements, such as logos, mottos, advertising, and store plans. The next step is what I call patterning. What are the components that overlap or connect historical chapters of different products, segments, and businesses? How is each of these visible elements stacked against the four strong code criteria (time tested, accurate and specific, proprietary, and relevant)? How do the individual codes work together? Some may enhance essential values and ideas. Others can undermine them.

TESTING THE STRENGTH OF A BRANDS CODES

Once you have completed a brand audit and identified clear patterns, icons, and possible code, how can you test the strength of the potential code? One way is to hide your brand name, logo, or all references to a particular product, thereby showing your brand's an advertising and marketing campaigns to unaffiliated or unbiased people. Based on the displayed elements (e.g., color palette, material selection, font, voice/sound/sound, and even location), check if they can identify your company. This is the ultimate litmus test for power brands built on clear, consistent, and proprietary code.

Even if your company has a robust and identifiable code and a strong position in the market, remember that the market is dynamic, and customers are always making new decisions. Loyalists can stay away and attract new customers over time in order for the business to be sustainable, grow, and stay relevant. The act of balancing between keeping customers satisfied for many years and attracting new customers who may have different expectations than existing customers is a problem for all companies. In the next chapter, we'll look at this and other everyday challenges and the aesthetic solutions to address them.

CHAPTER 4

DESIGNED TO LAST

> ➤ **AESTHETIC APPROACHES FOR GENERAL CONCERN ISSUES**

While no two companies face the same problem, growth and viability barriers tend to be recognizable patterns. And many of them are best addressed through what we call an aesthetic solution. Only 60 of the 1955 Fortune 500 companies remained on the list in 2018. Why are few companies able to stay successful? In short, the majority of companies are playing games they can't win. Like Yahoo!, the target cannot beat Wal-Mart in Wal-Mart games. Google games could not defeat Google. However, Yahoo! in contrast, Target maintains a relatively stable state by playing its own games.

Looking at classic business challenges, solutions are generally not found in business school case studies or best-selling business books. They are deeply and profoundly empathetic about what their customers feel and what they please, not what they buy or where they shop, and their vision of being able to enhance joy as a person, not as a shopper. Understanding. According to Clayton Christensen, a Harvard Business School professor of business and one of the world's top experts in innovation and growth, when buying something, we want to hire it and work. Helping (if it finds something), we look sexy for a date or put something tasty and healthy in our kids' lunch box).

If the product works, hire again (that is, buy again). If it fails, launch it. We buy things because no matter how mediocre and grand, they want to help our efforts succeed. In other words, people buy things, not machines. People are emotional and make decisions primarily based on how they feel from the purchase. The better they feel, the more aggressive and loyal to their products and brands. Christensen says that companies can miss (and fail) this and make product and marketing decisions based on the buyer's attributes (status, age, job, gender) and the wrong correlation with his or her purchase decision.

No matter what business you do, I, like all businessmen, advise you to incorporate your values, your character, your style, and even your habits into the equations as much as possible. Why buy? What kind of feeling do you want to evoke with your purchase? Why and how specific products and brands you prefer to achieve that feeling? What's wrong with what makes you fail? Your personal opinion is important to your business. After all, you are also a consumer, and you are your own expert. Being you and bringing all of you into the process is your biggest differentiator, and at the human level, your customers are the most responsive. Form and enhance the voice and value of your company, including your personal beliefs and personal preferences.

Taking yourself to the table will deepen your empathy with your customers. Understanding is an important aspect of continuous improvement in aesthetics and business. A clear example of the lack of empathy is found in the launch and rapid disappearance of Google Glass. Google Glass did not fail or be fired by consumers due to insufficient investment in technical R & D, marketing, or communications. It failed because of how its basic design makes the wearer feel (unpleasant and unpleasant). I didn't want to see people wearing glasses. Google did not do the job.

THE COMMODITIZATION TRAP

If selling a product generally seems complicated, try selling the product. Your only benefit may be your relatively low price, and this benefit will necessarily decrease over time. However, some companies have made the seemingly insolvable challenge of selling simple, non-differentiated, replaceable products unique by designing entirely new and exciting human experiences based on outcomes. We have successfully transformed it into a differentiated and sustainable value proposition. We call this strategy a Starbucks solution to shift the focus from low-value products to high-value products. Whether they sell coffee, soy, or cement, such merchandise companies create a unique and exciting experience, and through aesthetic strategies that weave a rich story about the product to develop enthusiasm, desire, and loyalty. You have the opportunity to transform your entire business.

Unlike traditional coffee shops, Starbucks designed interiors with an emphasis on comfort over efficiency, built server varistors, and reminded us of European know-how and craftsmanship. The point here is not whether Starbucks is differentiated and relevant today. He asserts that his business has not evolved, but can be learned from his first breakthroughs and years of success. In the 1990s and beginning 2000s, Starbucks was recognized as a highly differentiated and innovative product. (The same is true of McDonald's in the 1960s and 70s.)

THE RUT OF THE RUNNER-UP

When the company comes in second, it is competing with excellent players with much deeper resources and skills. Such companies have joined or have joined companies that have established practices and traditions, sales and marketing techniques, and reputation for well-known companies. The hurdle is to combine appreciative purpose into your business in a way that enhances and differentiates your brand from industry leaders and attracts entirely new customer groups. For example, Southwest Airlines has grabbed your bag while being smart with its own design theme (just a machine without a heart), the inclusion of warm colors (Canyon Blue and Sunflower Yellow), and previous slogans, it is on. A typical example of retailing is, of course, target vs. Walmart. The goal could not compete with Wal-Mart, especially in terms of daily low prices, but it's cheap and chic strategy has effectively built a strong position in the market. Designer partnerships; clever and catchy ads. Provide a community.

Excellence spark Clinique is an added symbol of a company that has built its own strong position, avoiding competition with market leaders. Clinique was launched in 1968 by Est Lauder Companies and was designed in contrast to Est Lauder, one of the most established and popular sister brands in American department stores at the time. Although the two brands belonged to the same parent company, they were very competitive and sold similar products to the same buyer at the same store. But in terms of aesthetics, they could not be different anymore. Estrada focused on the elegance of the Old World and showed classically beautiful models in glamorous environments. Clinique, who emphasized the technical advantages, had never used the model in advertising. His product itself was a star. As such, it was carefully displayed by legendary photographer Irving Pen, artistically photographed, and appeared in an elegant and catchy campaign. You even took the line seriously, even with a name suggesting a French hospital.

Clinique's concept was born out of Carol Phillips, Vogue Beauty Editor, who believes in a more scientific three-tiered approach to skincare. While Lauder's beauty adviser was expected to create elegance and style, Clinique's adviser wore a lab coat and took a healing approach to customer training. Clinique has also built abacus-like devices for counters. The clients could diagnose their peel type: oily, dry, delicate, or federation. Last, whereas the Lauder spark was built on its powerful redolence's, all of the Clinique stocks were exchanged as allergy tested and fragrance-free.

THE WEIGHT OF HISTORY

In general, a deep legacy is a valuable asset for companies, but some companies are immersed in the past and lose all relevance to the present. The challenge for such companies is to integrate an aesthetic that revives the glamor and appeal of the brand while using the most influential historical codes. Sears and Strobe Breweries Company are examples of failed legacy brands. In the meantime, Gucci, Harley Davidson, and Hennessy flourished through many successive incarnations.

Sears' turnaround plan has nothing to do with aesthetics, imperfect retail, restructuring, and property management, and results in significant miscalculations in managing its core problems. In early October 2018, Sears prepared for bankruptcy. The problem with the Sears case is that it is a poor retailer, says Neil Saunders, general manager of Global Data Retail. Frankly, everything from retail to service to merchandise and basic business standards has failed in all aspects of retail.

Sears management has overlooked the human element of business by closing stores and auctioning real estate to lower costs, increase cash flow, and make profits. If the Sears problem was simply over inflation, the strategy might have made sense. But having too many stores isn't why Sears suffered from it. Branch sales in the fourth quarter of 2017 decreased from $ 6.1 billion in the fourth quarter of 2016 to $ 4.4 billion. The company itself believes that half of these losses are due to less space. The remaining loss results from an 18% decline in sales in the same business. 11 Sears continues to sell its inventory and is looking for buyers of different brands who may drop IV drops a little longer, which will revive the store.

The truth is that Sears has become independent of consumers. To highlight this point, a 2016 survey of women's clothing buyers found that they preferred to shop in the Good Will Store rather than Sears. And people choose to shop at Amazon because it is related to their needs for convenience, accessibility, ease of use, and transparency. Amazon is the only version of the thick 21st century Sears catalog that families had previously received in the mail and is only available around the clock. Like today's Amazon, Sears catalogs cover everything from garden fabrics to prefabricated houses and celebrities like Lauren Bacall, Susan Hayward, Jean Autry, and legendary baseball legend Ted Williams. Products. Although Sears' product range has declined significantly since its heyday, Amazon is still reaching the limits of what can be sold. The storage system and the cooperation between humans and robot technology can store and send a variety of items. The partnership with the manufacturer means that there are no longer many other items to be offered for sale. In the case of Sears, it failed to replace aesthetic intelligence with financial engineering.

NO ROOM TO ROAM

What is the artistic process to build a new, captive, and loyal customer base despite the competitive pressure and the noise on the market? The challenge for most startups, especially in the small consumer goods sector, is to compete in increasingly crowded, competitive, and mature industries. However, several new companies, such as the eyewear manufacturer Warby Parker and the clothing brand Eberlane, were able to resolve the chaos.

At the time of this writing, Warby Parker is valued at approximately $ 1 billion. It's prominent today, but four business school students wondered why glasses and small pieces of plastic were so expensive. Answering this question has inspired selling fashion specs at a much lower price. Luxottica, the same company that owns the leading lens manufacturer of eyewear, owns Pearle Vision, Ray-Ban and Oakley, and licenses for all prescription eyewear frames and sunglasses for Chanel and Prada and many other brands. Name glasses. The founder of Warby Parker believed that avoiding retailers and their intermediaries could save consumers the 300% surcharge associated with selling drinks in stores.

For those looking to buy designer eyewear brands like Chanel, Luxottica pays royalties to the brand and increases retail prices by an additional premium. The popularity of branded glasses has given the founder of Warby Parker great tips for success in the glasses business. You have to pay attention to the wishes of the customers in order to achieve a high level of experience when buying glasses. How do customers buy drinks? First and foremost, check if they look good on your face. So, we're the first co-founders of fashion brands, and Neil Blumental told Forbes. The glasses are fashionable and fun, and the buying experience is incredible. Order 5 frames, and they will be shipped free of charge. Then try it on, ask your friends what it looks like, choose one and send it back with your recipe. A few days later, new glasses receive a fraction of the retail price. And while the price certainly speaks to the annoying question that everyone who wears glasses often asks (why is this plastic lump so expensive?), He's brought Warby Parker into its own segment. These brands cleverly create moments of customer experience that differ from traditional value propositions for players in highly competitive areas. Your commitment goes well beyond the design, features, and capabilities of salable products. It is based on experiences that promote a sense of community, curiosity, and buyer relationships.

AN INDUSTRIAL DILEMMA

This series of challenges affect companies with industrial products that are manufactured and sold for their utility. Above all, people who buy such goods want them to be practical and durable because the exchange of such goods is expensive. Most of us don't have to replace SUVs every year. There's no need to install an oven every six months or paint the living room on a 60-day schedule. Some companies such as Dyson (vacuum cleaner), Viking (stove), Yeti (cooler), Harrys (razor), Benjamin Moore (color), and Porcelanosa (floor tiles) are asked to use aesthetic models. Creating brands that are valued is much better than the properties of the product.

Because the aesthetics of use is so essential to Dyson, we recently announced that we would no longer develop plug-in vacuum cleaners, but would focus our innovative efforts on the versatility and functionality of cordless devices and robots. Many of us know that the vacuum cleaner cable is wrapped around the table legs, sucked into the mouth of the vacuum cleaner, and stumbled over it. Annoying. This even prevents many people I know from pulling the vacuum cleaner out of the closet, unless this is essential for their well-being. Cordless vacuum cleaners and robotic vacuum cleaners, in combination with Dyson's powerful suction technology (the first function sold, a vacuum cleaner that loses no suction power), have benefited from cleaning people and homeowners everywhere. The company has really come to our rescue and wants easy and quick cleaning and maintenance. This is the epitome of empathy when creating a product. Not because it's easy for Dyson, but because it's easy and fun for customers to clean.

The beauty of Yeti is the ability to make usual camping, hunting, and fishing accessory cooler a real wish. The product is so effective (hungry grizzly bears don't break into the cooler when they're closed), and customers boast of the company. You do marketing for us. But Yeti isn't really about coolers. It is about protecting nature and nature. About sportiness and wilderness. This brand was founded by Ryan and Roy Ciders, who wanted to start a fishing rod company. It was first sold to serious fishers and hunters, a hobby that their brothers also enjoy. The so-called hook and ball masses use the more refreshing function almost immediately to protect their contents and keep them fresh and crisp for much longer than the competitors of long-standing industry leaders such as Coleman and Iglu.

With spare parts, the company also helps consumers with the problem of sending many buyers of other coolers to the store to make a full replacement. Replacing a $ 500 more relaxed because parts become unusable doesn't look suitable for companies that rely heavily on consumer confidence. The cooler is designed so that fragile items can be replaced quickly and easily. At home, the dog chews on the [rope handle] and informs the customer instead of sending a replacement cooler. Hey, take out the slotted screwdriver, jump out, and that will fall. Ryan sends a new one. But is the ability to keep beer and fish fresh for hours is worth the price ten times higher ($ 300 to $ 1,300 versus $ 25 to $ 150 for competing brands)? No, the ability of siblings to create authentic brand stories became more critical for success than the non-destructive nature of the product. History has helped grow into a $ 450 million company in less than 20 years.

THE ETHICS OF AESTHETICS

As parents of two teenagers, we are concerned about the temptation to attack them every day. One of them is steaming. Technologies that are superficially designed to help adults quit smoking are products and behaviors that develop, especially for teenagers and teenagers for their own enjoyment. Juul is the most advanced company in the areas of design, marketing, and experience. Even the name (pronounced jewel) suggests something precious and desirable, especially for young people. However, the name also refers to joules, the amount of energy needed to generate one watt of power per second. Products like Apple and Thumb Drive are offered in different spot colors. Then connect it to a USB port on your computer like a flash drive and activate it.

Aesthetics can fail. This is not because its use at the sensory base level is not fun or exciting, but because the aesthetic is deliberately misleading or misleading or is intended to attract customers. This is known as the junk food effect. This product may be desirable and taste good, but it does not nourish the body and does not leave a pleasant aftertaste. There is also a strong claim that junk food is named for a reason. Worse than a lack of nutrition, eating consistently over time can affect your health.

Capitalists and entrepreneurs alike should have a conscience. Aesthetics are powerful and can backfire (and commercial) in terms of reputation if your business strategy is to take advantage of them. One example is Juul, a company that is now partly owned by the leading tobacco manufacturer Altria. In October 2018, the FDA unexpectedly stormed an office in San Francisco and confiscated more than 1,000 documents related to marketing, sales strategies, and product design that were particularly attractive to teenagers and other young people. This was done to guarantee that the organization complies with federal regulations for the sale and marketing of products. This is worrying as the use of e-cigarettes among teenagers increased with the decline in traditional smoking. In 2017, about 12 percent of students and about 3 percent of middle school students used electronic cigarettes, but about 7.6 percent of students smoked regular cigarettes. Juul was successful, but how much does it cost? And do you want your tween to adopt habits?

CHAPTER 5

TUNING IN TO TASTE

Appreciation for style and aesthetics is not innate. It has to be developed and refined over time. And there are standards for quality and beauty. Just because you don't like Bordeaux wine doesn't mean you can't tell the difference between good and bad wine. You can. The more you learn what is right, the more you can appreciate it, even if it does not fit your personal hobby. The most obvious way to understand how the taste evolves is to study how the feeling of a particular food or drink changes over time. In this chapter, we use taste - the sense of taste - as a metaphor for the concept of a broader taste - the perception of aesthetic excellence.

Eating is a necessary experience. Everyone does it. What affects the taste of food, not just the ingredients, but also the environment, attitudes, memories, expectations, and company (the number of delicious meals that became digestible when the meal contained controversial food mates)? There are many. The taste increases or decreases with the nutritional experience. Understanding how this works is a window on how the taste can be developed and improved in the broader sense of words.

The taste of food and drink is formed between the sensory nervous system and different parts of the brain and, like most other nerve functions, is improved and sharpened the attention, exercise, and experience. Historically, scientists believed that the human nervous system was fixed, and neurogenesis (the growth of nerve tissue) was stopped after the embryonic stage. However, in the second half of the 20th century, researchers discovered that neurons continued to form throughout life, reshaped the brain, and made new connections through experience, conception, and even sensation. For example, most children like to eat ice cream, although they are not taught to eat ice cream. Sweetness, richness, and creaminess are inherently fun.

In contrast, children do not usually enjoy the taste of coffee or alcohol. However, these drinks are very attractive for many adults. In contrast to ice cream, both coffee, and alcohol gain taste. Your pleasure comes from exposure and cultivation. They provide clear evidence that taste changes, and many flavors develop and are learned.

Some exercises and activities can help promote and promote taste development. However, the first step is to be committed and patient. Good taste develops over time and is influenced by a variety of factors, only a few of which can be controlled. Personal preferences are primarily shaped by time and place, not only by living conditions but also by individual circumstances such as education and family values. It is also made up of genetics. For example, some studies suggest that our genes determine whether or not they prefer the taste of coriander.

THE FLAVOR OF FOOD—A TROPE FOR THE REFINEMENTREGARDING LIFE

When we think about how to go on a diet, we learn about the variety of tastes and how we can adapt to them. Needless to say, how and why we move away from sensory experiences. Training yourself to become more aware of it is an important (and usually delightful) step in aesthetic development. The exercises and principles described here can also be applied to other sensory activities. These principles show how specific artistic experiences, expressions, codes, and decisions work, why some combinations work well, and others do not.

The concept of "delicious food" is misleading. Of course, you will experience food through taste. This biological function is the primary way to recognize sweet, salty, bitter, sour, and umami sensations. We also experience food through our culture, taste expectations, memories of the past, and new information and ideas about what we eat. When communicating information about diet, taste must be considered not only scientifically, but overall. It is not enough to reach a consensus in a room full of tasters that a particular dining experience is desirable or undesirable. It is essential to understand all of the factors that promote individual awareness.

EUGENICS AND APPRECIATION

In fact, our DNA determines most of what we taste and whether we like or dislike what we feel. Studies show that 41 to 48 percent of our food preferences are genetic. The human tongue has 2,000 to 5,000 thousand of flavors. All flavors have 50 to 100 receptors that process five taste profiles: sweet, salty, bitter, sour, umami (often referred to as savory). DNA determines the number of receptors. In Asia, South America, and some parts of Africa, 85% of the local population is a very sensitive taster (especially bitter compounds), and indigenous Europeans are less susceptible to different tastes.

Researchers have also found that those who hate hearty foods have more flavor than usual. That is, the taste approaches or exceeds 5,000. Scientists call these people "super starters." These people can register characteristics much more sharply than others and often have an apparent aversion to super-sweet foods, strong coffee, fatty, and spicy barbecue sauces and hop beers. If a gene makes up almost half of some taste preferences over other flavors, what determines the other half? And how do experience, exposure, and effort shape the other half?

OTHER SENSES, OTHER QUALITIES

All our senses begin to work when we eat. Sight Smell Touch Taste Sound: Sybil Kapoor, a British food writer and author of A New Way to Cook, is looking at how food stimulates a variety of sensations. `` The fluffy feel of peach skin, the fresh smell of basil, the sharp shock. In her book, she's essential to recognize how temperature can change the taste of food. She suggests that iced coffee is not as bitter as hot coffee, as she responds more to bitter tastes like hot coffee. Cheese Monger will tell you this: At least one hour after removing the cheddar wedge or Camembert wheel from the refrigerator, and you will actually experience the subtle flavor layers offered by various cheeses. Recommended to sweet, salty, nuts, milky, lawn, etc.

Even the way food is sliced its taste. Thick slabs of roast beef are gamey and chewy, while slices of paper cut into meat grains are softer. Similarly, a thin slice of Thanksgiving turkey breast is dry, made of paper, and unflavored, while the whole breast is cut thick and diagonally, making it juicy and buttery. While biting Parmesan cheese chunks, you can focus on the grainy texture instead of the salty nuts.

Enough of what we contemplate discrimination is actually smelling. Kapoor suggests picking up fresh laurel leaves, crushing them by hand, and feeling the damaged leaves. Unmistakable herbal essences comfortably remind you of winter dishes and hearty soups. However, when you taste the leaves, you can see that they are very bitter and feel worse. The same applies to vanilla extracts. It smells of God, but drinking a bite proves bitter and harsh. Many people like the smell of garlic crushed for sauces and other dishes, but the taste of raw garlic is exciting and stinging.

CONSCIOUSNESS AND ESSENCE

Our individual DNA has to do with how we perceive and enjoy the taste, but nature is not fully controlled. How we are introduced to food in our families and communities, and the messages we receive about the food around us also make a difference and exceed our natural prejudice. When preparing food, peeling, slicing, mixing, and sautéing rituals evoke a variety of memories of home, childhood, romance, fun, eaten meals, and gatherings. Food and taste preferences are closely tied to personal experience—the feel, taste, smell, and appearance of food cause strong and meaningful emotional associations. I've seen this in terms of how the shape, thinness, clarity, and quality of wine glasses affect the taste of wine.

CULTURE AND REFINEMENT

Our tastes continue to evolve, in part, through the introduction of new multicultural foods and flavors. As the world becomes more connected, and people travel and travel more comfortable, flavor preferences that were once considered local have grown, and demand for new flavor profiles has grown. According to

Cristle Kuhurst, an international food industry consultant for a UK-based marketing clinic, many countries maintain a very strong food culture but are also influenced by external influences.

This is not surprising to any of us. Try eating national and regional dishes. You can see that there is much academic debate about where it started. "Is the pizza born out of Naples when the ancient Greeks and Egyptians all ate as many breadless toppings as we know? All the dishes are available with local food. It is a fusion of gender, external influences, and historical evolution, and this evolution continues today: cultural influences such as films, fashion, and health messages affect what we eat. It's evolving, not being done. We're all part of this evolution, "says Lukehurst.

This evolution explains that modern Italian teenagers prefer American-style beer over Italian wine. Wine has strong Italian roots and rarely disappears from the Italian menu. However, the choices made by Italian teens are influenced by cultural influences such as American pop culture, says Lukehurst. You. Italian teens increasingly drink beer in situations where their parents were drinking wine or water. As demand for American-style beer in Italy grew, beer companies began to move to satisfy it. "It may be fair to say that [beer makers] are actively pursuing the teen market, but it will definitely meet demand." But millennials and up-and-comers in many European countries, Generation Z drinks less alcohol, such as beer and wine, than the whole parent. "They haven't acquired alcohol preferences in their teens and early twenties, and don't feel the same needs they saw in earlier generations," says Lukehurst.

In China, coffee, once a nearly completely different beverage, now represents a rapidly growing competitive market. Domestic companies are also actively participating in major US powers such as Starbucks. Similarly, as China's production methods have become more sophisticated and consumer preferences have expanded, the once-existing Chinese potato chip market has grown exponentially over the past two decades. A significant player in the Chinese chip market is known for developing unusual flavor chips with a regional twist (New England Lobster Roll, Cajun Spice, etc.). We do the same thing in China, adding a popular flavor to the chips. Durian is a thorny green Southeast Asian fruit.

In the United States, the most crucial restaurant food trends for 2018 include African and Peruvian flavors, rare herbs such as probate and lemon balm, ethnic breakfast foods such as chorizo scrambled eggs, and coconut milk pancakes, sambal, Indonesian hot sauce and jag, Yemen cilantro sauce. Of course, food producers will change the flavor profile of these and other ethnic foods to make them more delicious or accessible in culturally different markets. We went to Rome, and we know the difference between the pasta sauce we got in the city and the red spaghetti sauce we ordered from an Italian American pizzeria. The food you buy on the streets of Shanghai is quite different from what you'll find at a Chinese buffet or takeaway in the Midwestern United States. However, even if these foods lack the reliability of taste, texture, and appearance, there are enough markers or codes that can be identified by inclination and a recognizable flavor profile.

BACK TO NATURE

Information and education also create new desires for different flavors and foods. For example, consumer demand for more natural and organic local foods, i.e., moving from farms to tables, has led to a better understanding of the impact of industrial foods on our bodies and has been marketed as "natural." What you actually taste, see, and feel natural.

77

The way foods are processed effects which flavors we crave. Genuine or "whole" foods contain varying amounts of protein, fat, fiber, water, and carbohydrates (although unprocessed animal products have no carbs). As the food is processed, these ingredients are modified or changed in some way: concentrated, increased, or decreased. Food prepared with added sugar and salt is addictive, and food manufacturers know that. They have found a way to bypass the body regulators that tell us when we are full, stop eating, and instead increase our desire for mainly sugary, salty foods. This has changed the way we interact with and respond to flavors. Many of us (remember, most of us are not "supertasters") need more like a sugary, salty taste to satisfy their desires. And we are often not satisfied until we eat multiple "servings" of a given food-the result of manipulating food and flavor.

As much is now written about how much sugar and salt are added to processed foods, consumers have noticed that these additions manipulate the food they crave-and they Say he does not like it. But it also works: the sweetness of food has increased while other flavors such as bitterness have almost disappeared. Rediscovering tastes like bitterness (Campari on rocks, arugula salad, sautéed rapini) is another way to awaken our senses and broaden the perception (and appreciation) of various tastes. All of the ways we experience food and taste, including assumptions about what we eat, taste, and how we respond to the experience, are informed by everything I just discussed and other factors. Your mood, the weather, the place you were hungry, and who you are with. Several circumstances are included in the method of developing taste, so you need to make sure that the most critical factors are recognized.

KIND: DOING GOOD WHILE SNACKING

The story of Daniel Lubetzky, the founder of the fruit and nut snack food "Kind," is informative. Lubetzky, the son of the Holocaust survivors, founded Kind in 2004 to be more Kind to the world in the form of healthy snacks. The company has proliferated. Of the approximately 2,000 products in the nutrition bar category, six of the top ten best-selling products are type bars. In fact, Kind has become the fastest-growing energy and nutrition bar brand in the United States. In 2017,

Mars, the world's largest snack company, invested in Kind and valued the company to $ 4 billion.

Kind's success is based in part on Lubetzky's original mission to spread kindness. This concept not only differentiates your brand from traditional competitors but also raises awareness and sparks meaningful dialogue with consumers. One strategy was to distribute plastic cards to employees of the company to reward kind acts. If they see someone engaged in a kind act, such as abandoning a seat in the subway or helping the elderly cross the street, they give the card to a delinquent. Next, Kind sent Good Samaritans two Kind bars and another card to tell the kindness to someone else. Called a "non-profit," the company promised thousands of dollars for customer-generated projects that return to the community. However, Kind is differentiating beyond marketing messages and tactics. The package is designed for maximum clarity with clear wrap, so consumers can see the essential ingredients of nuts and dried fruits and easily imagine the taste and texture of each bar before chewing You.

Varieties could also take advantage of the changing dietary habits of Americans. It was not just the luck of the brand. The idea was to use aesthetics to increase customer sensitivity.

During the 1990s and early 2000s, energy and nutrition bars were considered a specialty purchase and were sold extensively to athletes and dieters. Currently, the more common customers are looking for healthy, convenient snacks made from real, minimal materials that are transparent and labeled without the use of many preservatives. Approximately 27 million Americans ate the health bar in 2013 by creating products using natural ingredients and creating packages and messages that enhance their aesthetics. I don't think Kind Bar is much healthier than any other snack bar-it has much sugar. But they are somehow tied to words that reflect pure and overall health.

AESTHETIC EXERCISE: THE ART AND SCIENCE OF NOTICING

It is possible to train to be more conscious about what we eat or experience more widely, and how we feel about such feelings and why. The more you become engrossed in the experience, the more critical you will notice the key factors that make your eating experience better or worse. You may eat out quite a bit, but how often do you pay attention to all the details? In a Harvard class, a teacher assigned students a restaurant review selected a restaurant and explained the dining experience so that readers who had never eaten at the restaurant could experience a meal at that restaurant. They encouraged them to focus their evaluations on the most precise and most noteworthy elements as clearly as possible. Their students learned how much they noticed during the dining experience, how correct the particular venue was (and was wrong), and how the non-taste stimuli (quality of lighting, ventilation, sound, etc.) The perception of food surprised how they formed.

CHAPTER 6

INTERPRETING (AND REINTERPRETING) PERSONAL STYLE

In the previous chapter, we talked about taste in the context of food and flavor. But aesthetics is gratitude for all senses, and aesthetic intelligence is to understand how and why a sensation causes certain emotions, delightful emotions, through all forms of stimulation. In this chapter, we want to learn about personal things and talk about how to start the process by cultivating and expressing one's aesthetics, depending on appearance and style, individually what and how to wear.

After all, good taste comes from the inside, and what we call the "4 Cs": clarity, coherence, creativity, and confidence show the right style. Does your appearance show a clear sense of who you are, what you care about, and how your inner self is connected to your outer persona? Do others associate you with some consistent style or fashion markers or "codes" according to previous brand discussions? Creativity is found in the uniqueness of the code. Are they identifiable markers? And is your most robust system unique, original, and memorable? Working towards these Cs will not only help strengthen your image but will also create a valuable skill set to build business interest.

Many people consider "fashion" as frivolous or generous. Figuring out what to wear is often considered a "first world problem" and seems to overlook those who cannot afford to invest much money in the wardrobe. The most fashionable people are not people who have money. Somewhat, extreme wealth reduces the ability to edit choices, make thoughtful trade-offs, and maintain discipline. These are the three essential elements of the right style. Our concern about the style is the misconception that we are limited to specific social clusters—for example, a fashionista in his twenties living in a cosmopolitan area. We look at people of all socio-economic segments and in all cultures, young and old, men and women who are interested in their appearance and present themselves in a unique and exciting way.

Humans have an intrinsic urge to decorate themselves in some way, from tattoos and piercings to jewelry and colorful fabrics. We do it not only to please ourselves but also to get the attention of others. Decorations of all forms differentiate us, express our ideas of beauty through humans, and symbolize the need to assert our status and what we aim for. It has a long history. In 2004, shell beads were unearthed from four sites in Morocco. These sites seem to confirm that early humans wore symbolic jewelry as early as 80,000 years ago. These beads were added to similar archaeological discoveries dating back to 110,000 years ago in Algeria, Morocco, Israel, and South Africa, confirming that these are the oldest forms of personal ornaments, and inherited own ornaments. It shows that there is a common tradition through culture over thousands of years.

INTELLIGENCE ATTUNEMENT WITHIN STYLE

Attunement with another person is when you can communicate without saying a word and still be understood by facial expressions, facial expressions, blinks, or raising eyebrows. While posing in yoga classes, jogging in the park, and browsing in the bookstore, when we are fully involved, we focus on what we are doing at that moment. We are adapted to those experiences. In food, attunement is the ability to identify the layers of taste in a dish and evaluate how the wine you drink affects the taste of the food and the surrounding atmosphere (lighting, table settings, music, etc.). -It affects the overall dining experience. In personal style and fashion, attunement comes from paying attention to how different methods, such as color, fabric, and fit, make you feel.

Today we often talk about "in the moment" or "fully conscious" and explain attunement. For example, if you are lying on the beach on a hot summer day, you may feel the warmth of the sun on your skin and the rough sand on your feet. You may also feel the smell of sea salt in the air. Most people experience these sensations with pleasure, but some of the associated experiences-such as the feel of a tight wet swimsuit or a bite of careless seawater-are not at all comfortable. The more you get used to the physical environment and its sensations, how they affect your body, and how you feel about their effects, the stronger the foundation for developing AI.

As with much of AI, our body is a better guide than our mind when it comes to seeing the effects of all these sensations. Tobacco dripping from the lips or being pinched between two fingers was actually a statement of fashion. Most people do not enjoy their first cigarette experience. The difference between addicts and me is that they endure and eventually develop a whole new set of emotional responses to the same physical sensations. Ultimately, they crave for smoking habits and nicotine addiction.

Applying attunement to personal style and "fashion" often starts with a keen understanding of your body. How do you want your clothes to look at your organization? It may determine the shape and silhouette of your choice. It may also indicate a particular color or pattern (or lack thereof). How do you want your clothes to feel in your body? It may guide you in choosing materials, textures, and fits. People have gone through their fashion stages in search of personal style, but they have all contributed somewhere to where we finally landed.

DRESS CODES

Dress codes exist in almost every situation. Offices have dress codes (sometimes institutionalized through the Employee Handbook), casual and formal ("black tie") parties have dress codes, and weddings and funerals have dress codes. Often, these codes are set according to cultural conventions or contextual empathy. For example, you don't wear a low-cut evening dress at a funeral or a white gown at a wedding (unless you're a bride).

Fashion codes work similarly to how brand codes work. Most of us wear suits or modern versions of suits (jackets, shirts, pants, or skirts) in corporate offices, and on weekends we wear sportswear (T-shirts or sweaters, slacks), and we What to think (amplified colors), sparkling or sparkling, more accessories) when attending a formal event. The different approaches to dressing can be divided into two clusters: uniforms and costumes. If you look at a man in a suit, he's obviously doing some administrative work. You might think of it as an "office worker" or "manager." Uniforms are worn every day and are consistent and predictable, even with different colors of ties and shoes. Costumes work to enhance externally set dress codes, but generally, impair personal systems and individual styles.

Weekend outfits also tend to fall into a uniform category. Whatever you do to do business on a Saturday morning, it will not feel comfortable for you to wear to the board. But there are differences in weekend wear—recognizable codes of status (more on this later) and personality. People wearing Brooks Brothers polo shirts and khakis imply that they are different from those in rock and roll group T and torn jeans originating from secondhand clothing stores. Costumes may be worn on a Saturday night, but it may change radically from time to time as

88

individual events are our `` peacock moments " and show off our personality, desires, and talents.

Breaking the dress code is one way to convey aspects of your talent and personality. Architect Peter Marino, who designs most of the boutiques of Chanel, Louis Vuitton, and Dior around the world, describes his day-to-day work as a "leather architect." If you looked at him and didn't know that he was a respected interior designer, he would, thanks to his leather attire and numerous tattoos, find a 1980s leather bar scene on the west side of Manhattan Would be an ancestor to That is precisely his preferred method. In fact, he refers to the "decoy" perspective. He broke the code of the architect's look: simple, unobtrusive, and traditional. From Frank Lloyd Wright to Frank Gehry, its dress code is basically unchanged.

CULTURE, STATUS, AND STYLE

Personal preferences do not develop in a vacuum. Some of them (and both dislikes and dislikes) are the environment in which you grew up, what you observed during your growth and development, what challenges you face, and what you need to solve. Come from a problem that must not be, some aspects of the style come from the time we live in, such as the influence of technology and media, and some come from geographic details. If you don't fit your style, you can reject the cultural impact of time and place. The best personal methods don't follow the trend and aren't interested in being "fashionable."

We also know that clothing has long been used to differentiate the status and power of different people and to improve class differentiation in many cultures around the world. Before the democratization of fashion in recent decades and the transition to a more homogeneous and casual look, the choice of clothing as a means of skipping social class. If you come from the lower level and have bought a nice suit, you can pretend to be away for a professional company. Says the infamous (and currently rehabilitating) fraudster Frank Abanale Jr., painted by Leonardo DiCaprio in the 2002 film "Catch Me If You Can."

In the late 13th century, the representation of wealth through clothing became common in Europe, and places of human life could easily be identified from their clothing. Clothing means background, culture, morality, wealth, power. From the 19th to the early 20th centuries, cotton pants, dungarees, and T-shirts were reserved for workers, but today the rich are deliberately torn (and very expensive). It often appears in blue jeans and expensive and whisper-thin cotton t's. Outsiders who are not familiar with the modern fashion code can look at such clothes and not think about one of the drivers of society. Tattoos were once a state of coastal residents and a state of motorcycle gangsters. They are very famous among actresses, soccer mothers, and architects who have seen them. Forbidden, not hidden tattoos often occupy the center of the red carpet as an "accessory" for attractive evening dresses.

In ancient China, yellow meant to center and earth, and only the emperor was allowed to wear it. Large layers of turban and clothing made of expensive and essential fabrics were reserved for the nobles in Africa, ruled by Hausa. In Japan, stories were told about the social status of the wearer, depending on the color, weave, style, size, and hardness of the kimono.

HOW TO LOOK AT CLOTHES

If you take your personal style development seriously (or want to improve or change your current look), you have to look at your clothes and try them on. Please experience it sensually. Fashion designer Kay Unger says: "If you just bring it into the locker room, you don't have to buy it." The only requirement for trying on clothes is wearing appropriate underwear. Clothes look very different on hangers and the human body. It looks very different, even in a human body, without essential clothing to adapt to the contours. The structured dress requires a foundation to hang and fit correctly. "The biggest suggestion is not to be afraid to come out of the box," says Unger. "Find the signature. It's a clear and recognizable detail of your style," she says. "It was a pin for Madeleine Albright. Michelle Obama sleeveless accepted, and the belt was her wonderful signature." The signature is an accessible path to personal style. Even if you have to wear a suit every day at work, professionals can sign. "Wear a colorful suit," says Unger. "Or if you feel like you have to wear black or dark blue suit, you have to wear colorful blouses and shirts.

CHAPTER 7

THE ART OF CURATION

> ➤ **RESTORING HARMONY AND BALANCE**

Curation is one of the words that people often use without knowing exactly what it means—the term associated with the treatment or restoration of the name. As you curate your business, you not only eliminate things that aren't working (and distracting or harmful) but also put things that work comfortably and successfully. Curing or curing is not just about reducing or removing. It also means assembling what remains in a fun way. In the aesthetics business context, curation restores the harmony and beauty of a product, service, campaign, or store design. In this chapter, we'll look at how to influence the choices you make to your customers, how the experience of drawing in space affects your bottom line, and finally, how to hone your curation skills, Explore the Curation Process A unique personal space that reflects your preferences and values purely, using a process that can be applied to your business.

The Italian outer brand Moncler was founded in 1952 by René Ramillon. The name is derived from the origin of the Monestiers Clermont, a town in the Alps near Grenoble. Early products included quilted sleeping bags and tents. The company's first down jacket or hoodie was introduced in 1954 and was devised as a way to protect factory workers from the cold. French mountaineer Lionel Terrey saw the potential and helped develop his exploration expertise. The same year, the jacket was used when the Italian team climbed K2. In 1968, Moncler was used by the French ski team at the Grenoble Winter Olympics. Effective against the elements, the appearance of the first hoodie looked like an unshaped bag. By the mid-1990s, the brand was struggling financially and overtaken by other prominent outer lines, such as the high-end Prada and the more affordable sporty-end North Face. The company was sick and needed treatment.

In 2003, the brand was acquired by Italian creative director and entrepreneur Remorphini. Morphine came from a long and famous line of Italian textile manufacturers and business people. At that time, the company's turnover was only about $ 60 million, bleeding money. Under Rufini's leadership and curation, the brand has grown from a simple, boxed goose down jacket to what the French call la doudoune chic (chic jacket),

Italian, il-piumino di Lusso (luxury down jacket). Did. In 2008, Carlyle Group, a private equity company, acquired 48% of the company and became the largest shareholder. As Carlyle's Managing Director, he joined the company's board that year (and remained on the board until 2010). It aims to help the company enter North America and other non-European markets.

In 2013, the company was listed on the Milan Stock Exchange. Carlyle sold its shares over the years, generating one of the company's top returns from its European funds. Today, Moncler employs more than 1,000 workers and causes close to $ 2 billion annually. It is also the first outerwear brand to demonstrate fashion authority.

So how did Rufini use aesthetics to curate or cure the company? He maintained a high-quality finish and detail. However, he modernized the style of the product and incorporated more fashionable high-tech components. He also expanded the product line (boots, hats, sweaters, etc.) without ever throwing away his core product, Parker. Unexpected collaborations with renowned designers such as Thom Browne, Junya Watanabe, and Giambattista Valli have added vitality and fashion to the line. Hot fashion shows held at unexpected locations (for example, models posing along the scaffolding of Chelsea sea head in Manhattan, flash mobs of models at Grand Central Station, ice skaters around Walman Rink in Central Park)) Has brought extraordinary editorial coverage and positioning of the collection as a high quality but cutting-edge brand. The retail store rollout (today, there are more than 200 significant locations around the world) did not happen overnight.

Several books address the issue of "selection overload," where consumers take too long to make, decide, and make decisions. In the book The Paradox of Choice, Barry Schwartz shows that too many choices are detrimental to psychological and emotional well-being. Also, customers are more likely to give up trying to make a selection, which can negatively impact your business revenue. They are often frustrated with their choice (and brand) if they can manage to decide.

Similarly, Columbia Business School professor Sina Eienger focused on research on ways to help consumers make better choices. In many ways, her recommendations reflect the curation process. This is especially true when selecting overload. One of her studies looked at how people make retirement savings decisions, specifically how the number of retirement plan funding affects future savings potential. If only two funds were provided in the plan, the participation rate was about 75%. In the 50-funding plan, participation dropped to about 60%. The more choices, the more likely people are to give up trying to decide on one and only put all the money into a money market account, Iyengar found. This is not a wise decision in terms of future financial security.

As with most skills, you need to practice curation to gain the skills truly. Without real practice, you probably won't be able to get there. You can learn a lot about curation and compelling aesthetic stories through the process of interior design or how to compose a space based on personal preferences and needs. Even those who are organizing retirement plan options for their employees can benefit from this. The power of aesthetic intelligence is most evident in consumer products and services, but it can also be a significant differentiator for professional service companies.

CURATION, OPPORTUNITY, AND THE DECEASE (AND REBIRTH) OF THE DEPARTMENT STORE

Department store owners are always designing spaces with the customer in mind. But recently, the aesthetics of traditional department stores have lost their advantage. According to the U.S. Census Bureau, retail formats have declined for decades, with a share of retail sales falling from 5.54% in 1998 to 1.58% in 2017, making redesigning the shopping experience a business imperative. Consumers today rarely consider visiting a local department store as a treasure hunt. They are not interested in lingering and browsing. They do not have the luxury in the process of discovery and surprise. They now want what they want and are not very tolerant of the long waits and news that their sizes are out of stock. The idea is to get what they want and get out. Old model curation and traditional customer service are less important. Digital retailers such as Amazon and Wayfair continue to develop, and perfect algorithms that prioritize consumer convenience and predictive purchase choices, curating their experiences as well as physical store departments Are under pressure. Offer to customers.

Fortunately, there is still a way for department stores (and other physical stores) to succeed: providing customers with an important reason to step into physical space, offering fewer but better choices, etc. Could you encourage them to spend money? They also need to give a more energetic perspective on who they are and what they are for (and what kind of customers they want to reach). Presenting a unique perspective does not satisfy everyone, but it is not the point but will resonate with the most loyal customers. Aesthetic retailers also need to provide exceptional service. They need to be serious about serving others and invest in hiring and developing staff with knowledge and know-how. All of this comes from the intent and need to create profound, immersive advanced experiences that cannot be easily replicated in other stores and certainly cannot be replicated online. Offline retailers must find ways to be more agile and bring freshness and surprise to shoppers. To do so, prioritize structural curatorial interventions and more meaningful metrics such as length, engagement, and memory, and look for older, more successful sales, such as sales per square foot, retail conversion rates, and average sales per order. Needs a difficult suggestion of throwing out the indicators—relationship between in-store experience, purchase decisions, product satisfaction, and tendency to return.

CURATING EXPERIENCES

Changing products frequently and reducing choices are two promising strategies for retail success. Another is to create an enchanting environment that provides entertainment and enlightenment. Some favorite offline stores are 10 Corso Como, Dover Street Market, and ABC Carpet & Home. The first two have carefully selected locations around the world. The third is based in New York City. Each is successful through mindful curation. It sells many of the same categories of products and brands as large stores such as Bloomingdale's and Barneys New York but sells them in a way that makes shopping fun, exciting, memorable, and desirable. Also, rather than creating an encyclopedia-like an online store or offering as thoroughly as a traditional department store, the curation of offerings based on specific sensitivities allows customers to choose Easier to do. They do not provide everything to everyone. They focus on a distinct type of customer and offer only the very best options.

Interestingly, Bloomingdale in the 1980s and Barneys in the 1990s provided an equally exciting shopping experience. However, none of the stores had exclusive merchandise or fancy displays decades ago. Initially, it was not possible to maintain the quality of the "destination."

10 Corso Como is based in Milan, Seoul, Beijing, Shanghai, and New York. In 1990, former Vogue Italia fashion editor Cala Sozzani called it a `` virtual story, " with a focus on art galleries and bookstores. Established. It feels like a lively breathing magazine with identifiable editorial options or curation in food, fashion, art, music, lifestyle, and design. A shopper or visitor learns, understands, and displays objects in context. Customers use the product in such a way at home. We recommend touching, holding, and trying on. The curation of the products offered are also unique: international, often craftsmanship and handmade. It does not show the same ones offered by other department stores. Not only is it special and enjoyable to walk around the store, but you can't source the same product on Amazon using your smartphone. Avoid the so-called showroom effect that has hurt traditional retailers in the past few years. Besides, all this aesthetic surprise is achieved at about 25,000 square feet. This is about 20% of the typical department store size.

Dover Street Market similarly presents brands and ideas in narrative form. The display is lively and original. They tell stories about products, their designers, and potential customers. Founder Kawakubo Re told reporters. "We want to create a kind of market where creators from different fields come together and meet in a beautiful, chaotic atmosphere. A personal vision."

In one area of the London store, the hats are on a pile of banquet chairs that overlap each other, creating an almost wood-like effect like a sculpture. You pull out a lid from one of the "branches" of the chair to try it on. The Nike Shop, a shop in the shop, is uniquely organized and displayed. Of course, you can buy Nike workout wear online, but with the ingenuity of Dover Street Market, customers will be able to buy on the spot. Shopping Nike is even more experiential because it can double as an event space.

Dover Street Market breaks many local rules for displays. It differs from the traditional way of loading a hat on a random pile of chairs or aisles made by garment racks that are ubiquitous in most departments, combining a variety of stacked and suspended goods. Stores that use many unexpected display strategies, such as creating aisles through display structures. The result is a unique exploration experience combined with a unique product set that reflects both the aesthetics of the store, the aspirations of the customer, and the hunger for novelty and surprise for convenience and "friction-free" shopping.

EVERYTHING IS PERSONAL

The process of curating your personal space will help you prepare to make better curation decisions in your business. Like all muscles, curatorial skills are developed through exercise. Besides, once you have a strong sense of personal style-the clarity and accuracy of what makes you feel good and feel inadequate in your life, you can apply understanding and identification to your business. With the right curation, you can build trust with your customers.

When designing and managing a home, office, retail space, or product, you need to keep your users in mind. As it is mentioned, the more you understand how to use space (or how to dress and dress), the more you can empathize with others. In interior design, you need to consider who takes up space and how to use it. When you actually use an area, you need to curate the design elements and objects you place in the space. Put them down. How do you like living and feeling in space? Don't be too dangerous. Nothing is as unpleasant as a strictly tense space. Humor brings cheap relief. It helps you relax and connect. It is an essential part of conveying many kinds of messages, especially in designs that include sophisticated designs.

Jonathan Adler built a business based on this idea, incorporating whimsical figurines and ironic motifs into his products.

AESTHETIC EXERCISE: MOOD BOARD

As suggested earlier, mood boards are a useful tool to start the curation process. An array of images, materials, textures, text, and other visual cues intended to capture a style, concept, or feeling and set the creative direction for a particular project or idea. The mood board has three powers. (1) Enforce choices and trade-offs. Specifically, which elements to include on the board, and not equally important ones. (2) You need to study and experiment with the relative placement of the components on the board. In other words, they determine how the pieces combine to form a cohesive and compelling story. (3) Provide a platform that connects visual and other elements with the emotions you are trying to recall.

The first step in curation is to always collect ideas and inspiration in the form of images, words, textures, and materials. This gives us an accurate picture of what we like and how the components interact to create stories and messages. Editing, the second step, is often much more difficult. Decide which entries to keep or which to skip. The third step is related to placement. Where does each input, contextually, fit in relation to other factors?

The power of the mood board lies in the way it combines everything, not just the images you select. Rather than relying solely on stock photos and pictures, use old photos to look for textures (metal chains and sisal links, paint swatches, small stone slabs, etc.). Don't be tied to consistency. Look for contrast and dimensions. How do the opposites work for each other? As you begin to place one next to another, you may find that you need to edit it further. Some choices have been eliminated, and many ideas have been modified and refined. What makes a mood board work is thoughtful editing and meaningful juxtaposition that tells a good story, conveys a clear message and elicits strong emotions.

CHAPTER 8

ARTICULATING ARTISTRY

Let's suppose you have an outcome that attracts several senses. One is well-designed and relevant to the purpose. A right product that meets the aesthetic criteria described at this point (robust code, multi-sensory activation, intelligent curation) should not sit on a shelf and wait to be found. Customers and stakeholders (team members, vendors) need to quickly and easily see, feel, experience, and understand code and other forms of communication, intuitively appreciate their benefits and assets and spend enthusiastically. This is achieved by articulation. An articulation, one of the critical skills that facilitate capture and acceptance, articulates and articulates the product's aesthetic strategy and ideals (including benefits) through words, storytelling, and/or other forms of communication—ability to convey. Articulations are made by visual impressions, but also by marketing and messaging. Each has an aesthetic sensation.

As noted throughout this book, good design is critical to the success of any product or service. However, the most common template for articulation, a "concept brief," is as important as the product or service itself. This document is a guide for writers, visual artists, designers, merchandisers, and others to plan and produce creative work on product curation. Define target consumers and provide blueprints to reach them. All parties must understand creative briefs. Internal staff needs to know how to use it, and consumers need to enjoy the summary language—an "in-house" guide with an "outward" purpose.

The art department can create these briefs, but often the task is left to the hands of the executive responsible for the process, ideally the CEO. The best leaders do not delegate these activities to bystanders. In fact, they are invested and familiar with the creative direction of their business, as they do in analytics, financial, and operational functions. Steve Jobs is believed to value Apple product aesthetics and design as much as features and sales strategies, but his pragmatic approach is still considered an outlier. As I have discussed here, the separation of "business mind" and "creative mind" is more feasible than ever. For this purpose, it is prescribed that all specialists, not just "creative workers," briefly explain the aesthetic strategy of the product. In this chapter, we will dig more in-depth with some examples of how some leaders have begun to adjust the business of aesthetics and the business of profits.

THE VALUE OF WORDS

The priority of aesthetic clarity is specificity. It is essential to communicate your purpose, give meaning to your product, and evoke strong positive emotions. And teams can understand, duplicate, improve, and execute their visions. The specificity not only guarantees the accuracy of the expression but also creates a more unique, powerful, and memorable connection with the product or service. For this purpose, every word you choose to describe a brand or product is essential. Ambiguity is not acceptable. For example, words like beautiful, tasty, and soft are common adjectives, while words like slouchy, salty, and gelatinous represent information accurately and clearly. The words you choose should recall your experience with the product (or service).

Tim Lomas, a specialist in positive psychology and intercultural lexicography at the University of East London, says that many words convey a particular emotional experience in different languages that have no English equivalent. He believes that learning this knowledge will improve understanding of the nuances of human experience. If so, learning new ways of describing human experiences help pinpoint those experiences and relate them to products.

Lomas says that the first time he learned the Finnish word sisu, which is an exceptional determination in the face of adversity, he was inspired by the search for words that have no native English equivalent. The Finns say that English words such as "grid,""patience," and "resilience" do not justify the deep inner strength that the Seth conveys when used by voice actors. Other words in Lomas' lexicographical list include Arabic, a state of musically induced ecstasy. Yuan at (Chinese), perfect and complete sense of achievement. Sukha (Sanskrit), true permanent happiness, regardless of your situation. And longing, a strong desire for another being, even if it cannot be reached. The Lomas site contains many other untranslatable words.

For each word (or sentence) you use, answer the following questions to determine the correct choice:

➤ **DO YOU DESCRIBE YOUR PRODUCT IN SUCH A WAY THAT SOMEONE ELSE IMAGINES THE SAME IMAGE AS YOU?** Are you accurate? For example, Burberry's signature fabric is not called a "plaid." Tan, black, and red tartans are known as "hay market checks." KFC doesn't say fried chicken is "delicious" but means "licking a finger" is right. Besides, the original KFC represents Kentucky fried chicken, not southern fried chicken. Why is it important? Founder Harland Sanders wanted to differentiate his restaurant from all its southern competitors. At that time, Kentucky products were exotic and evoked an exceptional Southern hospitality style.

➤ **ARE THE WORDS "OWNABLE"?**In other words, can they quickly and uniquely identify with your product? For example, when you hear the phrase "the happiest place on earth," you think of Disneyland. When you see the tagline, "Just do it," you think of Nike. The same goes for Maxwell House Coffee's "until the last drop." Even more potent than "owning" expression is the ability to own words. IBM has historically carried the word THINK. Today, Google "owns" word search.

Careful word selection will also promote the desirability (and sale) of individual products. For example, McDonald's is not just selling traditional hamburgers and breakfast sandwiches. I sell Big Mac and Egg McMuffins. Similarly, Ben & Jerry flavors are "ownable" flavors, such as cherry Garcia, chunky monkey, coffee toffee crunch, rather than the general description of chocolate, vanilla, strawberry, etc. In cosmetics, Narus's best-selling pink peach blush is called "orgasm." Launched in 1999, this product was a hit from the start. We say that customers have fallen in love with the name as much as they were shade. Tom Ford's latest scent is not only fabulous but also fucking fabulous. It sells well at $ 804 for 250ml. Which woman in the world would not want to be so considered by her affection?

To settle down on the right words to describe your company or product, you need to understand your audience. What do they feel before they encounter your product? What do they tell themselves about the quality your product may have and the benefits it may offer? Describe the emotional experience you want to provide to the product. What do you want customers to feel when interacting with your product? What do you want to remember?

> **IS THE LANGUAGE YOU WANT TO USE CENTRAL OR ANCILLARY TO THE EXPERIENCE YOU WANT TO PROVIDE?**In many cases, when writing a dissertation, students would write a complete description on the page, but it was worth paying attention to only some of them. (Note that he had to score more than 100 dissertations, so he was particularly frustrated by outside efforts.) The aesthetic expression is not only accurate communication but also sturdy and attractive. It is a typical and memorable expression. Boilerplate, boilerplate, and business speech do not promote your case.

For example, consider that most cable companies are notorious for eliciting positive emotions through communication. For example, if you visit the Xfinity website, you'll see detailed but funny references to subscription packages based on features such as Mbps downloads, channel counts, and pricing. This site is full of data but lacks voice and personality. The company appears to see customers as machine service buyers, rather than real people looking for entertainment options. Not surprisingly, Comcast has historically had the worst customer satisfaction of any US company or government agency. In 2014, it was named "The Worst Company in the United States" by The Consumerist, a consumer blog that is now obsolete. In 2016, Comcast paid a $ 2.3 million fine to resolve a federal investigation into a claim that added fees to customer bills, including unordered services, boxes, and digital video recorders. 2017, J. Both D. Power and the financial news site 24/7 Wall Street have named Comcast the worst company in the United States.

> **DOES YOUR WORD MAINTAIN THE OVERALL TONE YOU WANT TO SET FOR YOUR PRODUCT AND COMPANY?** Do you want to enhance your company's value, not just its product attributes and aesthetics? Consider the national anthem of the cooler-maker Yeti. A few miles past the last traffic light. What is there is that you are beside the rebellious spirit that bets the truth and goes one mile further. Like you, they believe that wherever you want to be, nowhere is too far away. "These words reinforce the idea that they make products

that can be used every day can withstand aggression and harsh weather conditions, and care for people with broad physical and emotional boundaries. The tone matches the aesthetic intent of the product.

WHY ARE YOU HERE? THE ANECDOTE

Narration, beyond individual words, defines phrases that include storytelling, history, company traditions (and myths), founding principles, reasons for existence, and instructions and instructions. Recently, most companies and product websites have an "About" section. People want to know whom they are doing business with. For companies with a long and long heritage, such as Tiffany and Chanel, history and lore are an essential part of storytelling, establishing credibility and trust, and passing information on to the next generation. That would be their mother or grandmother.

Relevance is also significant for an established brand. That's why the Tiffany website has a section on sustainability and responsible mining practices. Whether or not you agree with the sustainability initiative, the company is still keenly aware of the issues surrounding sourcing and processing diamonds. In contrast, companies like Sears / Kmart have much legacy and have proven to be unable to communicate relevance to their customers. Who would really miss them when Sears and Kumart completely disappeared? If you cannot show why your product or company needs to exist, you are doomed to disappear. Also, few people notice or care when they go out.

For new companies, compelling narration, especially in the mature sector, is reshaping what consumers want to buy and creating demand that did not previously exist. This is achieved by emphasizing key differences from existing products, superior value over what is available, and unique benefits that consumers can't get anywhere else. Of course, a new company will attract us with novelty and playfulness, or sophisticated technology and style. This is a tribute to its newness. In this way, innovation can be presented as an advantage (new and exciting) rather than negative (new and untested).

PICTURE THIS

Appearance is important, especially if the thumbnail pictures on the computer screen are likely to be the first to be seen when the customer encounters the product. More than ever, the images and packages you choose to enhance your product, including real illustrations and photos, logos, packaging, and marketing materials, need to be strengthened, duplicated, and adjusted. The product itself like words and images, tones and textures, moods, and personalities—these need to work together seamlessly.

Do the images you select reflect the personality and mission of your business? Do visual cues and pictures show creativity, feel authentic, and show what the brand expects? Also, all visual information must resonate with the target audience. If fun is a fundamental emotion associated with your brand, do people's images convey that emotion? Are the colors used fun? Does the package enhance playfulness? Virgin is a good example. Logos like the company's signature look like founder Richard Branson graffitied on a napkin. It's your edgy face, like Branson's own bold, rustic, and yes, fun personality. Nickelodeon, a television network, also feels good, thanks to the balloon-like typeface set on orange splatter. Orange itself is a fun colour, combined with a playful shape, is really lively.

Images and visual cues must also be consistent. This way, like the selected word, it is owned and associated with your brand. It needs to span all touchpoints, including websites, ads, in-store displays, and social media posts.

IT'S A WRAP

Packaging design has an immediate visual impact on consumers. In essence, it is a multi-sensory experience. In a new field of research called " neuro design ", the packaging stands out from the crowd, how it contributes to brand loyalty, and how humans can elicit certain behaviors and emotions of consumers. Try to understand what can be used for brain function.

Some of the most aesthetically pleasing products are packaged in containers of their own beauty, separate from the product itself, and encourage consumers to store and reuse or display the package. This was once true for a small number of items, such as perfume bottles and sometimes sake bottles, but now includes things such as glass candle holders, makeup containers, and canned tomatoes. When the original products are empty, they can each be used for anything else, such as storage or display. For example, Natasha Roller, a Virginia-based event planner, has specially ordered Bianco di Napoli tomatoes in Italy to use attractive, well-designed cans as flower containers.

Packaging needs to tell the story, and it needs to be done quickly. First impressions are essential. It must cause a positive emotional response to consumers. Besides, if there are products sold by many other companies, they compete with them both for shelf space and attention. Sufficient packaging helps convey product benefits, value, and differences from other options in a crowded market. Above all, it can elicit and strengthen essential emotions.

Color is essential. Studies show that nearly 90% of snap decisions made on products are based solely on color. Approximately 80% of consumers believe that color enhances brand awareness. Specific colors, such as black, evoke the drama and apply thoroughly to fashion brands such as Chanel and Gucci. Blue indicates reliability and is used effectively by American Express and Ford Motor Company. Greens are "natural" and rejuvenated. It is clear from the effects on Starbucks and Whole Foods.

ARTICULATING BEAUTY

Beauty products are often at the forefront of design and packaging. After all, in the world of makeup, moisturizers, and mascara, competition is fierce, and a particular brand rarely monopolizes product ingredients and formulations. Companies need to continually innovate both products and packaging to attract the attention of shop buyers, beauty editors, and consumers. Explicit expressions of the product are particularly important, as beauty customers tend to be loyal. If you find one that works, it's not easy to switch gears and try something new that doesn't work. Many (primarily young) customers tend to try and replace beauty products each time they change T-shirts, but long-term advocates bring the most value to cosmetic companies.

It's not that these standard players don't try new things. We are always looking for something that works better, smells better, and feels more fun. The original product means you need to be assured that it is worth investing in to try it out. Some brands achieve this through sampling and in-store product testers. Others have gained attention and trust through other assets, such as high-quality features and materials (that is, leather instead of plastic, crystal instead of glass, and brass instead of pot metal). The look and style of the people working behind the counter. Display cleanliness, order, consistency.

In the case of the skincare brand Philosophy, its introduction to the market was unexpected, and its success surprised the industry. We looked for consumers who are not the typical target market for beauty addicts and beauty product manufacturers. Cristina Carlino founded Philosophy in 1996 after developing another successful line of cosmetics called Bio Medic, sold through doctors 'and cosmetic surgeons' offices.

ARTICULATING THE DINING EXPERIENCE

Nix, New York's vegetarian restaurant, offers a two-seater rail-style banquet on the wall in front of the restaurant, or you can sit at a long freestanding indigo blue maple table behind the house You. Cork bars, potted green plants, and whitewashed Scandinavian walls create a summery atmosphere even in the midst of miserable and cold New York winters. James Truman, who once directed magazines including Vogue, Glamor, and GQ as Condé Nast's editor-in-chief, is a leading innovator in the concept of space and restaurant, skillfully expressing a chic yet healthy aesthetic at the same time. Warmly welcome and refreshing downtown.

Before opening the restaurant, Truman thought months with his chef, pioneer in vegetable-centric cuisine, John Fraser, and architect Elizabeth Roberts, who blended modern aesthetics with traditional design elements. Nothing escaped the team's eyes. The details of the grout color used in the bathroom and the cut and fit of the weight staff apron were scrutinized. "As an editor, I came to the design process of thinking more about stories, not about pure aesthetics. What is an overall account, and design decisions as a way to establish and enhance that story? "Says Truman.

"Some of the first conversations overturn the perception that vegetarian / vegan restaurants aren't fun, dating, or partying, but rather dour, a place without pleasure. There was no reason for a vegetarian restaurant to have such an atmosphere, except for its historical precedent, which, logically, was a kind of twist: why it was not necessary to kill animals Does the restaurant feel like a funeral, and the steakhouse feels like a celebration? It doesn't make any sense. "He also didn't want the restaurant to have a direction called the" Brooklyn Model. " Unfinished wood walls and floors, 19th-century countryside details, server uniforms from an old Western movie.

"It was a statement about real, non-urban, farm-to-table values, but it was everywhere and began to look like a hipster pose soon after, " he points out. "At the same time, a new model of innovative cuisine came from Scandinavia, whose design also displayed ingredients, but in a very thoughtful and architectural way." Interestingly, Truman said He points out that this repetition shares the value of design with modern Japanese design. He believes this will be the dominant design aesthetic in the coming years, especially for small restaurants. "The large
122

rooms are designed with the French brasserie and Las Vegas in mind."

ARTICULATING TRANSPORTATION

Vespa Scooter, J. D. Earn 72.1% on all 24 vehicles considered in the Power's Annual Resale Value Award. That is, except for rare and collectible vehicles, Vespa Scooter is more valuable than any other vehicle on the road. This is surprising given that they do not go very fast and do not even have the horsepower of a Harley or Honda motorcycle. Vespa's success may be due to its uniqueness. "Vespa is a luxury brand," says Chelsea Rammers, founder of Moto Richmond, Virginia, who sells scooters and motorcycles for Vespa and other brands. "Most luxury brands have competition. Vespa has no competition."

This is not entirely true. Other luxury motorbikes made by Honda and Yamaha are cheaper and exceed Vespa in the United States. The essential new Vespa, Primavera, costs about $ 3,800 and does not include taxes or dealer fees. The most expensive model, the 946 RED, costs $ 10,500, but some of that cost goes to a charity (RED) founded by U2 lead singer Bono to fight HIV and AIDS in Africa.

Still, no other scooter has the same prestige, reputation, or history as Vespa. If you look at Italian movies since the 1950s, you can see that the character is riding a Vespa. In fact, when you go to Rome and other Italian cities, you'll see a row of Vespas neatly parked next to the sidewalk. They are not only beautiful but also very functional with regard to maneuvering in narrow city streets. This use in both popular culture and real-life has led to collective unconsciousness. Vespa implies freedom, urbanity, sophistication, style, and fun.

Part of the appeal of a scooter is its attractive design, which is basically unchanged. They look almost identical to what you always have. The 1946 model was streamlined, and today's scooters look a little retro but don't look kitsch or old-fashioned. It is also metal, but competitors have long replaced expensive materials with cheaper plastic parts. They are, simply put, beautiful objects and last a long time. The Vespa structure has what is called a monocoque frame. This means that the bodywork is a frame. Most other scooters have a separate body panel attached to the frame. This structure is lightweight and rigid. The result is a very smooth ride, an attractive quality, especially when navigating urban asphalt and cobblestones.

WHO STANDS TO GAIN?

Beyond claiming the value of good design, we call for more severe considerations and discussions about whom we will satisfy and inspire with our products. Ethical concerns are clearly related. Because consumers want to know, it makes sense to think carefully about what we do and how we can communicate it. And they're frustrated by companies that don't care about them. According to a survey by the insurance company Aflac, around 92% of millennials say that they are more likely to buy products from ethical companies. Part of the brand's moral commitment to consumers (and the planet) is to communicate how products can help both the "better" (environmental or other social reasons) and the buyer. This approach is becoming increasingly important as we move from consumerism to consumer society.

Consumerism began after World War II and our economic situation, as the main economic activity of the average person in the 1970s changed from savings and fruit to spending on goods and services and in the hat. As mentioned at the beginning of this book, consumerism as a lifestyle has gradually waned after decades of constant rule. Many circles are greeted with doubts and light. The popularity of the minimalist movement is such an indicator as to the sharing economy and the growth of experience-based companies in response to people's desire to create lifelong moments and memories. We welcome this transition. We have too many things, and many of what we lack have meaning, durability, and artistry.

CHAPTER 9

THE FUTURE OF AESTHETICS

We seem to be increasingly living in two worlds. The other looks for human-centered interactions, emotional connections, and experiences that have been developed, especially for us as individuals. Digital services and digital presence may soon replace my auto mechanic, accountant, and the courier, but my hairdresser, massage therapist, and interior designer will definitely be gone (at least for a long time). This subdivision affects aesthetics, and aesthetics evolve. Cultural and demographic change naturally continues to influence what we feel beautiful about and what we reject as unattractive and undesirable. As we saw in the rise of social media, human activity continues to focus on what I call REM: relationships, experiences, and memories.

The desire to connect intimately, honestly, and personally with others have rejected some form of social media and signaled a new way of millennials and others that have been marked by immigration from so-called superstar cities. From New York and

Los Angeles to small towns that could lead to community building. "We have seen major city outbreaks in recent years," said Stephen Pedigo, a specialist in business and urban development, director of the Shack Institute of Real Estate at New York University. "The place contains ideas about what people in urban communities want, and small and suburban communities are trying to do it again."

This migration can be driven by advances in the economy (metropolitan areas are expensive to live) and technologies that enable people to work outside the metro area, but not many. Small towns thrive for human-driven creative reasons. Aesthetics, not automation, will continue to support and drive the growth of these creative communities. This means that people everywhere, not just in the heart of big cities, find and expect the high level of aesthetics of the goods and services that they want and need. If you can't find them, make them. Many entrepreneurs will start businesses with a full and clear aesthetic value. As existing companies can develop the artistic intelligence and skills of their employees, more and more people can offer the holistic and human experience they want, expect, and demand.

THE ENVIRONMENTAL CRISIS

Consumers are aware that they can no longer be satisfied with the environment. One way to exercise environmental responsibility is by paying attention to the products you buy. Use the economic power to drive change and make the world better or at least less toxic. A study conducted by Cone / Porter Novelli on corporate social responsibility (CSR) shows that consumers are interested in the manufacture of their products.

Of all the groups surveyed, millennials most often used word of mouth and social media to share information about companies that they felt were environmentally and socially responsible. As millennials become increasingly dominant business groups, companies need to prepare to ensure, promote, and support their environmental impact. And since millennials are skeptical of strange claims, they have to be so trustworthy.

Aesthetics can play a vital role in this initiative by creating a clear and unambiguous story about the company's policies and practices for green manufacturing, including the innovative use of recyclable or reusable packaging. Nestlé, an international food giant, announced in April 2018 that all packaging would be recyclable or reusable by 2025. Walmart and Werner & Mertz have made similar promises. Organic Valley Packaging, a milk producer, is already recyclable (or reusable). Patagonia, a sportswear company, calls itself an "activist" and specializes in helping the environment. We believe that the seventh-generation household appliance manufacturer has a similar social and environmental mission. Expect more handcrafted items in response to consumer interest in more social and ecological activities, more significant sustainability efforts, and products with less environmental impact. This will promote a more tactile experience.

DIGITAL EXPANSION AND THE TACTILE EXPERIENCE

Expansion and spread of advanced computer and "smart" devices. Increased automation in most areas of the car, household, and workforce. Cheaper and faster access to all data is the result of a 40-year trend, followed by a pattern of more than 40 years. Some people welcome high-tech experiences and products, and others reject it and bring a new twist to the concept of the "digital divide." We are not in the world of what we have and what we do not but in the world of what we want and what we do not.

Automation replaces jobs in many areas, such as farms, fast food, driving, and office work. However, new posts are being created in industries that require creativity, originality, and a human touch (literally fig-like). Born, that's why aesthetic intelligence, such as art, science, and business strategy, is so essential for the future of work. If you don't have artistic skills, both the digital and the handmade world may be out of reach. The limitation is that computers can and will create art and music. However, we believe that people will continue to build in much more advanced and exciting ways. Some are similar to "human privileges." Many will prefer creative materials made by people and hands and pay more for them. The tasks associated with building and maintaining complex interpersonal relationships, including careers such as nursing, sports coaching, and psychotherapy, are reasonably safe from automation. Here too, aesthetic intelligence is required as competition in these areas increases to maintain and improve the customer base of the services.

And with improved automation and computer learning, people are looking for more creative and personal ways to improve the quality of life. This requires objects with better physical properties that offer sensory pleasure and reduce the almost constant exposure to the flatness of a two-dimensional screen. The desire for ever more vibrant sounds helps technology companies create more realistic listening experiences. They also want more live music experiences. There is even more appreciation for digital products that offer an enhanced aroma/taste/touch experience and for non-digital products that provide a rich sensory experience. In fashion and clothing, sensory experiences can actually be woven into the fabric. Consider thick and thick knitwear or knitwear beside very soft and soft textures and textiles with mixed media (e.g., down-filled materials and embroidery in leather and quilted).

In food, unusual and unexpected ingredients (e.g., spicy or savory ice cream, even more intense, sweeter, more pungent, and sour flavors) push the boundaries of culinary innovation, but there is also a return to "comfort eating." It offers a warm, nostalgic feeling. Some choose foods from space-age like Soilent, but most of us want to experience a variety of sensations and novelties when we get together to eat.

In the meantime, the technology continues to evolve and become part of high-tech fitness clothing and other wearables, tracking steps, Body Mass Index (BMI), calories burned and burned, blood pressure, and much more. Technology also affects foods and beverages and leads to more functional foods that can improve health and mood. Recess, based in the Hudson Valley, is a forerunner of this trend. The water is infused with a non-toxic hemp extract that is said to have analgesic, anxiolytic, and anti-inflammatory properties. Drinks contain adaptogens, which reduce stress and are said to improve memory, concentration, and immunity.

The focus is on practical physical work to achieve physical fitness, in contrast to high-tech training such as massages, new forms of yoga, and other mental and physical exercises that improve the sporting experience. Death Metal Yoga is an excellent example of a class that includes beating, kicking, air guitar playing, headbanging, and heavy sweating. Fitness centers are also being built smaller and closer to customers in rural areas to become more personalized or niche-oriented. It means a small center for old and young population groups. Transgender or those who serve certain religious groups.

Focusing on small communities and their needs is a way for most companies, not just fitness companies, to become more competitive in crowded areas. Niche markets that serve different age groups and desires are becoming increasingly common, and their aesthetic decisions distinguish them. To compensate for the depersonalized society, consumers long for their personality to be recognized, which will lead to the next shift.

TRIBAL SECESSION

Using the word secession doesn't mean the country is divided into smaller nations. However, it can happen, but a lot of geopolitical experts and others, as the Brexit illustrates, and predict that it will be. Yet, we have seen the rapid growth of identity politics, tribalism, localism, activism, and unfortunate terrorism in response to globalization and as a threat to local culture, language, and way of life. More than ever, people are trying to belong to groups that represent mutual emotions, shared values and goals, and a common cause or ideal that examines belief systems. These forces are driven by social media and can undermine both democracy and dictatorship.

The growth of the "tribes" was driven by the age of hyper localism (and the rejection of global harmony) and the "micro dominant". "The choice of lifestyle that will lead to the creation of the brand. Brands that serve micro-communities (such as trans- or gender-specific people, religious groups, historically overlooked and overlooked groups) are not the authenticity, integrity, and transformation that consumers want, but can't always do it. Redefine retail by creating and experiencing creative products. Find it now. Tribalism is the most potent force in the world today. The community becomes tribal. Brands form tribes. Large companies are tribal tribes.

In business, this means that the two consumer desires co-occur. First, products are shown that address smaller, more specific group IDs. Some products convey a feeling for the global blended design that is influenced by access to various cultural influences. The amalgamation and amalgamation of cultural heritage create new hybrid groups and identities such as "tribal techniques" and "industrial chic." People form groups or "tribes" in other ways in response to the fear of the harsh, unpredictable reality of the outside world. From cozy blankets to products and services that approach security and create trust and comfort, Coco continues to be necessary, along with the bracket, to support this.

BLURRED LINES

As it is mentioned earlier, people will form groups driven by shared ideologies, interests, and beliefs, but frequently groups and group members will identify outside of conventional norms. There is already a blurring of lines happening between male and female; straight and gay; black and white; and young and old. As a result, more brands and categories once conventionally divided by gender or age will become unisex or offer unisex items and age-fluid products and services. The children's brand Primary offers basics such as T-shirts, leggings, pants, skirts, and dresses in bright solid colors meant to be worn by all children from ages zero to twelve; conventional boys (pants, Ts) and girls (dresses, skirts) items are marketed to all children. The Phluid Project in SoHo in New York City may be the first officially gender-free retail space in the world. At three thousand square feet, the bright white store with large windows and high ceilings is part retail space and part "experiential platform," according to its content director, Jillian Brooks.

The store, aimed toward gender-nonconforming and gender-fluid consumers, uses customized gender-free mannequins that show off unisex basics from brands such as Levi's and Soul land, along with more fashion-forward choices from Gypsy Sport, Skin graft, and the fetish-inspired latex by Meat. The Phluid Project also offers its own line of T-shirts and hoodies, adorned with slogans, including "Stronger together" and "One world." Part of its mission is affordability, so prices are generally less than $300. No Sesso ("no sex/gender" in Italian) is another brand that has taken the idea of genderless clothing to new and unique areas with its use of vibrant color combinations, methods of tying, stitching, and embroidery; irregular knitting; and billowing or highly tailored fabrics. The clothes work with various body shapes (male/female, short/tall, large/small) because they have convertible or transformable features. In other words, customers can customize the clothing in many ways to suit their shape and identity.

Forging positive human connections is a combined effort and has far-reaching implications. If done well, it can lead to richer brand experiences. But the onus is on creators to align their ideas with motives worthy of being experienced personally and profoundly. The modern consumer, no longer driven to accumulate material possessions, seeks depth, authenticity, and meaning. Therefore, the brands that will endure will provide purpose—one that extends well beyond commercial motives, and that unites and empowers the people touched by their products or services. In the end, that is what truly and eternally challenges, compels, and delights their consumers—any opportunities to care for and respect them not for their consumption but for their humanity.